Profitable Direct Marketing

Profitable Direct Marketing

■ Ros Jay

INTERNATIONAL THOMSON PUBLISHING EUROPE

I(T)P® **An International Thomson Publishing Company**

London • Bonn • Boston • Johannesburg • Madrid • Melbourne • Mexico City • New York • Paris • Singapore • Tokyo • Toronto • Albany, NY • Belmont, CA • Cincinnati, OH • Detroit, MI

Profitable Direct Marketing

Copyright © 1998 Ros Jay

First published by International Thomson Business Press

I(T)P® A division of International Thomson Publishing Inc.
The ITP logo is a trademark under licence

British Library Cataloguing-in-Publication Data
A catalogue record for this book is available from the British Library

First edition 1998

Typeset by J&L Composition
Printed in the UK by Clays Ltd., St Ives plc

ISBN 1–86152–145–6

International Thomson Business Press
Berkshire House
168–173 High Holborn
London WC1V 7AA
UK

International Thomson Business Press
20 Park Plaza
13th Floor
Boston MA 02116
USA

http://www.itbp.com

Contents

Diskette

The diskette accompanying this title features 30 forms to help you plan and run your direct marketing campaign. All the forms are set up as Microsoft® Word 6.0 documents to allow you to customize each form to suit the needs of your company. All the documents can be opened through the File Manager in Windows®. The document titles and respective page references are given below. Each document is saved in a separate file and they are labelled from tab01.doc to tab30.doc.

Introduction

What is direct marketing?

- Direct marketing is the marketing weapon of the 1990s and beyond. It is the most precise, targeted form of marketing on a large scale that there is, and it is also the most cost effective when it is done properly. Direct marketing is any form of marketing in which you deal direct with the customer without going through any intermediary such as an agent, wholesaler, or retailer. This includes:

- Direct response advertising, where you ask the reader to contact you directly – phone, write, clip the coupon and so on.

- Direct mail, which entails sending a letter directly to the customer or prospect's home or business address.

- Door-to-door marketing – putting unaddressed leaflets through people's letterboxes.

- Mail order, where you send out a catalogue of products directly to customers and prospects.

- Telemarketing, which involves phoning people either to sell to them or as a way of supporting other selling techniques. ■

Direct marketing, when done well, can bring in a huge amount of business very cost effectively. However, the initial outlay can be quite high for many types of direct marketing, which means that you run the risk of losing a lot of money if you don't think through your campaigns carefully. The thing is, you're dealing with such large numbers. The beauty of direct marketing is that you can reach thousands of people very easily. And get a very high response. But that can mean printing thousands of letters or brochures or catalogues or leaflets, and of course that can't be done for nothing.

The good news, however, is that anyone can learn to run an effective direct marketing campaign. The principles are the same whether you are running a small business or looking after the marketing operation of a huge organization. This book is all about how to master those principles, and make sure that every campaign makes you money, rather than losing it.

Why do we need direct marketing?

The way things used to be just a few decades ago, if you wanted to sell your product you would put your best suit on and go and visit your customer or prospect. Depending on where they were based, and how long the meeting took, you might visit five or ten people a day if you were lucky; often far fewer.

Occasionally you might write to a customer to secure a sale, but you would generally expect to visit them as well; letters were for arranging appointments and confirming orders, not for doing business. In any case, each letter would be personalized for the particular customer you were writing to, and that took time.

Then the telephone became popular. Most of your customers would have had phones and you could make appointments much more quickly than by letter. Sometimes you could even make a sale over the phone if the product was relatively inexpensive, or if it was a repeat order. But you were still expected to visit customers from time to time, if only out of politeness.

These days, business is conducted at a faster pace. Often, customers actively dislike the time that a visit takes, and would rather deal with you by phone. Long letters are very time consuming, so if you only expect them to fill in an order form and stick it in the post, you're saving them time. And you're saving yourself time. You can deal with a hundred customers in the time it used to take to deal with one. The biggest danger is that you lose the personal touch that helped to build customer loyalty in the past.

Modern direct marketing, however, brings you the best of all these worlds. You no longer need to visit customers; you can write to them quickly and easily, and you can phone them. And best of all, with modern computerized marketing methods, you don't have to lose the personal touch. Letters can still be personalized so that your customers feel you are talking directly to them.

Some products are more cost effectively sold through retailers, wholesalers or agents. But most products are suited to direct marketing, at least some of the time. There are some products that still require visits and product demonstrations; if you sell nuclear submarines you wouldn't expect to secure many sales simply by mailing out a catalogue. But a lot of products that you market by making sales visits can still be supported by other direct marketing techniques. Add-on products and maintenance contracts can be sold by letter, accessories by mail order, and related products by phone.

Suppose you sell cars. Sure, your customers will want to visit your showroom and test drive the car before they buy it. But you could sell them a new maintenance contract after a year by post, and you could attract new customers using direct response advertising. Maybe you sell office machinery. Some people buy computers in response to ads, others like to see them first. But even if you visit your prospects in order to sell to them (which is still a form of direct marketing, although it isn't usually included in any definition of it), you can still market directly to them after the sale. You can send them a catalogue of accessories, or phone them to find out what other products they might be interested in.

The principles of direct marketing

Direct marketing is all about communicating with customers in as targeted a way as possible. So if you sell lawnmowers, you want to communicate with all your potential customers without wasting time or money writing to anyone who doesn't have a lawn. If you sell petrol-driven lawnmowers, you don't want to spend your money on communicating with people who would only ever buy an electric lawnmower.

Modern direct marketing techniques are all about making sure that you get as high a response rate as possible to any advertisement or mailshot because you have targeted as high a proportion as possible of genuine prospects. It's about using bullets and not buckshot, and that is why it can be so cost effective. It also explains why poor, badly targeted marketing can be a dreadful waste of money.

There's another important aspect of direct marketing, which many people aren't aware of: building customer loyalty. You don't just want to win customers, you want to keep them. After all, winning new customers can cost up to seven times as much as hanging on to the ones you've got, so it's worth putting a lot of effort into retaining existing customers.

Direct marketing is one of the very best ways to make your customers feel special and looked after, and ensure that they want to keep buying from you. Not every communication is about selling. You can mail customers with special offers, send them Christmas cards, phone them to make sure their last order was delivered correctly, send them free tickets for exhibitions you are attending, and generally make them feel that they are important to you. All these techniques are essential for creating customer loyalty, and are central to direct marketing. This book is a guide to making the most of this aspect of direct marketing as well as being a guide to making the initial sales.

Making it all possible

The boom in direct marketing over the last few years has been a result of one thing more than anything else: the development of the computer database. It is now possible to store a vast amount of information about your customers and prospects, and their buying habits and history, and then to select addresses for mailing on the basis of this information. So you could mail only those people who ordered from you last time, only those who are within 50 miles of an exhibition venue you'll be attending, or only those who live in the south west and spend over £50 on an average order.

Information is the key to direct marketing, and computers are the key to that information. The basis of any effective direct marketing operation is the database, which is why the first two chapters of this book are concerned specifically with this subject. The database is the foundation on which you build the whole operation.

Once you have set up an efficient database, and have a system for keeping it up to date and adding useful information later, you can start direct marketing. The third chapter looks at how to give the right impression to your prospects and customers by projecting the best image, writing persuasive copy and and giving the most tempting offers: the creative element of direct marketing.

After you have mastered the basics of the creative aspect – and they are all simple to master once you know the techniques – you need to decide which is the best medium for approaching each customer, and the best way to make sure they feel looked after and therefore stay loyal. So the rest of this book looks at each direct marketing approach in turn and examines when to use it, and how to make it work properly. By the end of the book, you should be able to make any direct marketing operation run smoothly and effectively, and bring in far more money than it costs you to run.

1

Establishing a Database

■   This is where it all starts. Your database is the single most useful weapon you have in your direct marketing armoury; it will make every campaign run smoothly. But only if it contains the right information. This chapter is all about the type of database you need and what information it should contain:

■   What kind of database?

■   What information goes on to the database?

■   Keeping your database clean.

■   The Data Protection Act.

■   Building and maintaining your database.

Once we've established that, the next chapter will look at what to do with it to get the best from it.   ■

What kind of database?

You might have a simple manual card index system on which you keep details of all your customers. Or you might have a powerful integrated computer system which records all transactions, financial and administrative, with every customer. Or you may have something in between. Whichever you have, there are certain requirements it needs to fulfill.

Integrate your database

The most important feature of a marketing database is that it should be fully integrated with your financial and administrative customer databases. If you try to run a separate database in parallel you will have to spend a huge amount of time updating it and you will inevitably find that it is sometimes out of date.

This may sound like a minor problem, but suppose you phone a customer who is in the middle of a major dispute with your despatch department over the non-delivery of an important item. If you use a different database from your despatch department, your database may not yet have this information entered. You could phone up with a special offer, chatty and breezy, to find an irate customer at the other end of the phone with a problem you know nothing about. If, however, you share the same database, this information should be clear before you ever pick up the phone.

You also save yourself a good deal of work updating your information if any data entered by anyone in the organization is automatically available for everyone else. So make sure that your marketing database is the customer database for the whole organization.

Accessing information

Marketing is all about people, not transactions. The primary means of access to information on the database should be by customer name. It is, after all, the customers who are important. You may want to be able to look up information by product or by order date or by any number of other search criteria – and this is a useful option – but the search criterion for which the system should be set up is the customers themselves.

Having said that, the database should give you the option of searching and selecting addresses according to any of the information stored (we'll look at the details of what information you should hold in a moment). You should be able to pull out all the customers who have ordered at a certain time, attended a certain exhibition, made a complaint in the last six months or who fall into any other category or combination of categories that you want to contact.

It doesn't matter if you have only a very basic system, so long as you fulfil these functions. If you've just started out in business and have a relatively small customer base, you may even keep your records manually. This can work fine for a while so long as you keep them integrated with every other part of the business, and have access to all the information you need. Once you have enough cash to reinvest in the business, put it into computerizing your database. The sooner you do it the more work you save yourself later.

So the three most important features of an effective database are that it should be:

1   integrated;

2   organized by customer name;

3   accessible by any search criteria.

What information goes on to the database?

The more relevant information your database contains, the more useful it will be. This means it will save you time and money by helping you to target the right people, and only the right people, in every direct marketing campaign. It also means that you can analyse your customers' and prospects' behaviour in detail, which will help you to plan and target future campaigns.

The four types of information

There are four categories of information which you should hold to make your database as comprehensive as you need it to be, so let's look at each category in turn.

Personal details

Obviously your database needs to include all your customers and prospects by name. But this is not just a customer list; a database is far more than that. You need to record as much information as you can about all the people on it, to help you analyse customer behaviour. For example, how will you know that a certain product is almost always bought by people over the age of 50 if you don't know your customers' ages? And if you don't have this information, how much money might you waste marketing the product to 20-year-olds?

It is easier to ask your customers and prospects for some kinds of information than others, and we'll look at how to establish this kind of data in the next chapter. But for now, here is the type of information that a typical database would hold on each consumer customer and prospect:

- name;
- age;
- marital status;
- number of children;
- employment status (e.g. professional, white collar, blue collar, self-employed, unemployed, retired);
- income bracket;
- lifestyle (child, student, young single adult, young married adult, married with children, etc.);
- type of job (civil servant, retailing, media, etc.);
- credit status.

It helps to list the lifestyle, income bracket, employment status and type of job as a code for easy access to the information. You could attribute numbers or letters, for example, to each category. So under employment status you could use the following codes:

professional	01
white collar	02
blue collar	03
self-employed	04
unemployed	05
retired	06

This gives you a kind of shorthand to use so you can store a lot of information without occupying a great deal of space on a screen or print-out, and can enter data more quickly.

If your customers are business people rather than consumers you will need to store slightly different information. Here is an idea of the data you would expect to hold about business customers and prospects:

- name;

- job description (as it would be printed on a letter);

- department or section (as it would be printed);

- direct phone number;

- direct fax number;

- e-mail address;

- job code (sales, buying, accounts etc.);

- authorizer or buyer (i.e. ultimate decision maker);

- personal address data (where relevant);

- cross reference key to company data.

Address details

This is the next section of data, and it is essential for making contact with your customers and prospects. It is also important for analysing whether certain products and services are more popular with people in certain types of property, or certain parts of the country. Here is an idea of the information you should aim to hold on consumers:

- full address;

- type of address (rural or urban, own property, rented or council property, detached house, semi-detached, terraced, apartment, etc.);

- regional code (e.g. Scotland, north east, north west, etc.);

- sales area (if you divide the country up into your own administrative sections);

- media area code (TV or newspaper regions for advertising).

Obviously you will devise your own way of allocating codes depending on the most useful way for you. You might choose to code people's address area according to your nearest branch or office, or only to divide the country into four or five sections.

When it comes to businesses, once again you will need a somewhat different set of information:

- full company name;

- shortened version of company name;

- full address;

- main phone number;

- main fax number;

- e-mail number;

- telex number;

- type of company code (parent, subsidiary, independent, sole trader, etc.);

- parent company details (where relevant);

- region code;

- area of business (e.g. Standard Industrial Classification codes – SIC – mining, industrial, chemical, etc.);

- principal products or services;

- importer and exporter indicators;

- number of employees bracket (e.g. 1–20, 21–49, 50–99, etc.);

- turnover bracket.

Financial data

You need to know whether or not your customers can pay for your products, or are prepared to. Experience may show you that they never spend above a certain level on each order, or that they will happily pay for the top-of-the-range product every time. However, experience cannot show you anything if it isn't recorded on your database. Here's the kind of information you should store:

- type of account;
- date of first order;
- date of most recent order;
- average balance/order value;
- average payment time.

Of course you may not hold all this information on prospects who have never ordered from you; however you could have bought in some information or have some other indication of their likely financial behaviour.

Activity record

This is the section of customer and prospect history with your business. This tells you not what they might do, or say they will do, or show some interest in doing. This tells you what they have actually done in the past; the size of orders they really place, and the frequency, and so on:

- type of responses by code (not only orders but also enquiries, responses to surveys, offers, competitions and so on);
- dates of above responses;
- frequency of response;
- value of response;
- method of response (phone, fax, post, e-mail, etc.);
- details of any disputes, late deliveries, faulty products, etc.;
- date and type of all contacts with the customer or prospect: mailings, phone calls, visits, visits to exhibitions, etc.

So there are four key types of information you need to include on your database:

1   personal details;

2   address details;

3   financial data;

4   activity record.

Keeping your database clean

It is essential to make sure that your database is as up-to-date as possible. If it contains details of people who are no longer at the address or company they are listed at, or who regularly waste your time and money responding to free offers but never ordering, every mailshot or phone call to them will be wasted – an expense you cannot afford in either time or money. These people should be purged from the list.

If you have two entries for the same person, perhaps because they have ordered twice giving slightly differing details, you will duplicate mailings which generates extra expense and may well irritate the poor customer who doesn't want to receive two (or more) of everything. These customer details should therefore be merged into one entry.

Merging and purging are the two key activities in keeping your database clean and up to date. Some organizations set aside time and staff resources at regular intervals to clean up their mailing lists and databases. This means that the information is never more than a few months out of date.

However, ideally you need to minimize the duplications and wrong entries continually, as well as having a regular spring clean. Everyone who uses the database should update any entry they find is incorrect or duplicated at the time they find the inconsistency; don't leave the mistake to be picked up when you spring clean. Any entry onto the database should be carefully checked at the time it is entered against the original source of the data.

Merging

One of the most common causes of duplication comes when lists are bought in or added to the system. These are not picked up because they differ slightly – the wrong details are entered, or the customer used a different name, perhaps. Robin Hay of Antwerp Electrical Company Limited could turn out to be the same person as Miss R Hay of AEC Ltd. So this kind of possibility should be checked out when the details are entered. This is one reason why it is very helpful to include all companies' full names and shortened versions on your database.

Separate contacts within the same organization should be listed separately and not merged, however, since they are unlikely to pass mail around between them.

Purging

There are various categories of entry that you may need to purge:

- people who ask to be removed from the list;
- high credit risks;
- people who enquire but never order from you;
- people who have moved away.

If you are unsure whether to purge someone who has never bought from you, you can send them a reply-paid card saying 'Please return this card if you would like to stay on our mailing list.' Set yourself a date, say three or four weeks ahead, when they will be purged if they haven't replied.

Another way to keep your list clean is to send each customer an annual card, enclosed in a regular mailing, which has their name and other details printed on it. Ask them to correct any errors and return the card (you pay the postage to encourage them). Do this often enough so that anyone who has moved is still getting their mail forwarded.

You can also clean up your database by putting a return address on your envelopes and deleting the database entry of anyone whose envelope comes back to you. However, the Royal Mail cannot guarantee to return the undelivered letters unless you mail them by first class post, which will prove rather costly. Also, a return address makes your mailing look like the mailshot it is, which can deter some people from opening it.

The Data Protection Act

If you store any information on computer other than a person's name and address, you must register with the Data Protection Registrar as a data user. Anyone who you are storing information about is entitled to know what information you hold on them, and there are restrictions on disclosing information to other people (e.g. selling mailing lists) without permission.

You can pick up a form DPRI at main post offices, or contact the Data Protection Registrar at: Springfield House, Water Lane, Wilmslow, Cheshire SK9 5AX.

Building and maintaining your database

If you already have all the information you need on your database – great. But what if you don't? Perhaps you're just starting to build your database, or you have an old and inefficient system with little information beyond a list of names and addresses, and you need to upgrade it and collect all the information which your wonderful new state-of-the-art system will contain.

Don't worry. The next chapter is all about how to collect the information you need for a really useful, effective database, and how to use the information once you have it to get the best from your database.

2

Upgrading and Using the Database

■ Once you have a thorough, up-to-date database on your computer system, you can start to make it earn its keep. You can pull a huge amount of useful information from a good database and the more imaginative you are, the better you can target your customers and prospects.

The last chapter looked at the kind of information you want to hold on your database and which you can add to all the time as a result of enquiries, sales and so on. But sometimes you want to add new information to your database. This chapter is about how to add this new data, and how to make the most of it once you have it.

The areas covered are:

■ Adding new information.

■ Using your database for analysis.

■ Using your database for selection.

■ Your marketing strategy. ■

Adding new information

There are two main categories of information you can add to your database. The first is new names – new prospects you can contact and try to convert into customers. And the second is new information about existing database entries. Perhaps you hold only a list of names, addresses and customer histories at the moment, and you want to develop it into a more useful database with information about customers' lifestyle, income bracket, age range and so on. If this is the case, you will need to do some market research.

Expanding your mailing list

If you want to be able to phone, mail or write to more people than you can at present, you will have to acquire more names to add to your database. You could add basic mailing details only, or full database information, depending on where you get your information from. But whatever information you decide you want, there are two basic ways to get hold of the data: researching it for yourself, or buying the information from someone else who already has it.

Expanding your list for yourself

You probably have new enquiries and leads trickling in all the time from various sources – advertisements, word-of-mouth and so on. But every so often you might want to add a substantial number of names. You will probably – though not necessarily – have a particular reason for doing this. You might want to expand into a new geographical region, or you may have discovered that your products appeal to a particular type of consumer or business and you want to add a lot of names from that category. Maybe you've discovered that the lightweight briefcases you sell are especially popular with people who travel to work by train, so you want to target these people.

The thing is, you need to encourage these people to give you at least their basic contact details in order for you to be able to write or phone. But how? Well, there are several techniques for doing precisely this. What you are aiming to do is to persuade these prospects to identify themselves.

Direct response advertising

We'll look at the techniques for this later in the book, but direct response advertising is any type of advertising in which you ask the reader, viewer or listener to respond directly to you, rather than go to a shop or talk to an agent or broker of some kind. Direct response advertising asks the respondent to call your number, clip a coupon and return it to you, call in at your showroom or visit your exhibition stand. Once they make their response, you are in communication with them and can add them to your database.

You can collect the type of names you want by advertising in the right place. For your lightweight briefcases this might be in the magazines that rail companies distribute on their own trains, or on posters in underground train carriages or in taxis.

Special offers and competitions

Why not give your prospects an incentive to contact you? You can print vouchers as part of your advertisement, which require them to fill in their name, address and phone number and return the voucher to you to redeem the free gift or special offer. Or you can run a competition or a draw of some description. Once again, they will have to fill out their details or you can't contact them if they win. You could run the competition in conjunction with a magazine, or at your exhibition stand, or simply as an advertisement. Or you could arrange for one of the shops on station forecourts to distribute the competition details for you by keeping them beside the till for rail travellers to pick up.

Rented mailing lists

You can either rent or buy mailing lists from other people who have already built up a database. Buying in lists is an excellent way to expand your database, and we'll look at it in a moment. If you rent a mailing list though, you won't be able to keep the names or it to add to your database. Sometimes you don't get to see the individual names being mailed because the company that owns the list mails out for you. Sometimes they will send you address labels, but there will be checks built in to make sure that you don't copy these names onto your database (some of the names will be people briefed by the list owner to let them know if you mail them).

Rented lists, however, are cheaper than bought lists, and can be an excellent way to build your database yourself. All you have to do is to send out a mailshot with a good incentive to reply – a good offer, a competition, free tickets, vouchers or whatever – and you can collect the details of all the respondents. The only people you can't add to your database are the ones who didn't reply anyway. If you think it may take more than one mailshot to spur people into responding, you can always rent the list again (although, of course, there comes a point when it would be cheaper to buy).

For your lightweight briefcases, you might find that rail companies are prepared to rent out lists of season-ticket holders, which you could select by region or by length of journey, or by first or standard class ticket holders.

Buying in external lists

If you buy in lists of names and details from another organization, you will have ready-made information to feed into your database. The fuller the information, the more it is worth and therefore the more it will cost. There are two basic types of list you can buy in:

1   Compiled lists: these are standard lists such as the electoral register, telephone directories, registers of shareholders.

2   Responsive lists: these are lists of people who have responded to other people's mailshots.

When you buy in a list it will be for direct mail or mail order marketing, and you are going to be mailing the people on it cold. They have had no previous contact with you. So there is no more reason why they should respond to your mailshot than why they should respond to an advertisement, an insert in a magazine or a leaflet through the front door (door-to-door advertising). So consider the cost of these alternatives.

A direct mailshot of four pieces (for example a leaflet, a voucher, an order form and an envelope) can cost 25 to 30 times as much per thousand people who see it as a full-page colour advertisement in a consumer magazine, once you take into account production as well as mailing. This means that before you pay for a list of names, it's worth making sure that direct mail really is the best way to reach the people you are aiming at.

Often it is the best way; if it allows you to sell straight from the mailshot when you couldn't from a single-page advertisement, or if it means you can enclose samples or swatches that any prospect would want to see before making a decision to buy, or if it gives you scope to present lots of well produced colour photographs – these factors may well make it the most effective way to market your organization to new prospects. But you must think about it first; the response to a cold mailing will be much lower than the response when you mail existing customers, or people who have already made contact with your organization.

Compiled lists

Compiled lists, such as those from phone directories, mean you can reach just about everyone in your target market. However, you may not be able to identify them very clearly, so you may end up reaching a lot of other people as well. They are useful for targeting regionally and locally; if you want to mail everyone in a certain street, housing estate, postcode area or town, this is the way to do it.

The electoral register gives you a little more information to select names by. For example, you can buy in a list that includes only addresses whose occupants have changed since last year's electoral roll. This is very useful to businesses whose products appeal to people who have recently moved; businesses selling carpets or loft insulation or garden design services, for example. It will also give you geodemographic information about the type of neighbourhood (council estate or owner-occupied; typical household disposable income) names of 18–24-year-olds still living at home, and other similar selection criteria.

Responsive lists

Some people reply to direct mail and some people just don't. The ones who just don't will not appear on responsive lists, which saves you mailing them. People on responsive lists have made some kind of response to other products, and if you can find the right product match for your target market, you can get a very good response rate from this kind of list. Finding the right list is the challenge.

List owners can refuse to sell you their list if they don't want their customers to receive information about your product, so you're not likely to get hold of your competitors' mailing lists. This means you have to find a list of people who have responded to a different product from your own, but one that will appeal to the same market. You might be able to sell your briefcases to people who buy traditional umbrellas, or to the rail season-ticket holders we considered earlier.

When you choose a responsive list, you need to consider how it was compiled. Is it a list of people who have bought by mail before, or simply people who have responded to a promotion, or made enquiries but not purchased? How recently or frequently have they responded? Are they small or big spenders? Has everyone on the list placed an order in the last six months, or have some of them not ordered for five years? This kind of thing will make a huge difference to the effectiveness of the list. Here are a few points to consider:

- **How accurate and up-to-date is the list?** If it hasn't been cleaned recently, you could spend a lot of money mailing people who have moved since the list was compiled, or sending out duplicate mailings.

- **What information are you buying exactly?** The list must include contact names, and for business prospects it must also include job titles. People are far less likely to open an envelope which says simply 'To the occupier' or 'Chief Buyer' on it (would you?). So it's crucial to have names. As far as any additional information is concerned – lifestyle data, for example – only you know what information you need and what it is worth to you, but make sure the list contains what you want before you agree to buy it.

- **What form does the information come in?** It sounds obvious, but make sure that the information comes on disk and in a format that is compatible with your system, unless you want to spend weeks entering it all manually. Conversely, if you are running a very small operation without a computerized system, make sure you can get the information printed out.

- **Make sure you can test the list first.** Any reputable list owner should let you send out a sample mailing to make sure that you aren't wasting your money on their list. After all, a mailshot of, say, 50,000 is not a cheap exercise. The usual minimum test size is a random sample of 5000 names, although you may be able to negotiate a lower number. However, remember that the average response to an unsolicited mailing is only about one or two per cent, which would give you no more than about 100 responses at most. If the sample were too small the test would not give you a reliable result.

- **Here's a funny thing:** the response to test mailings is almost always higher than the response to the full mailing. I can't tell you why – there are all sorts of theories but no one has yet come up with a convincing one. You'll just have to accept it. It means that once you have done a test you should assume that the list will actually give you a response rate of about 10 per cent less than the test indicates.

Responsive lists also include what are known as lifestyle databases. These are databases of people who have filled in long questionnaires and have given permission for their names to be rented and sold. The kind of information they contain includes credit cards used, type of car, type of employment, hobbies and interests, and dozens of other selectors. The biggest lifestyle databases in the UK have almost four million names each, and the people who have volunteered this information about themselves are usually fairly responsive. You would normally expect to pay a set price per thousand names for each selection criterion. So if you wanted to specify four criteria – for example, age range, sex, and two different occupation groups – you would pay four times.

The most effective way to use a lifestyle database is to submit a sample of your own buyers to the list manager. Many of these are likely to be on the lifestyle database already, and the list manager can match their profile with others on the database and give you a list of similar people.

Business lists

These fall into the same categories – compiled lists and responsive lists – but there are a few additional points to consider if you are buying in lists of business names:

- Compiled lists will give you a lower response, but are useful if you are targeting companies of a specific size or market sector, especially if you want full coverage of the market.

- Compiled lists often don't give you an individual name to contact. In this case you will need to get on the phone and call the companies concerned to get the information you need. According to research, this can cost you up to £5 per call if the switchboard operator can answer the question, and more if you have to be put through to someone else (by the time you consider the administrative costs, cost of staff time, cost of unconnected calls and so on). The average connection rate is about 15 calls an hour to the switchboard, and fewer if you need to be put through.

■ Responsive business lists tend to achieve a much higher response rate. They include people who attend exhibitions, subscribe to trade magazines, go on training courses, buy business equipment (especially in response to mail order or telephone selling), buy business books by mail order, and so on. One of the most popular categories is people who subscribe to business publications, but remember to consider whether it wouldn't be more cost effective simply to advertise in the publication itself. On the other hand, you might want to select managing directors only, and then MDs from the subscription lists of several different magazines.

Choosing the best list

There are three main sources of mailing lists: list owners (or managers whom they appoint to administer their lists), list brokers, and list compilers.

■ **A list owner** might be a trade association or another organization with a list of their own customers and prospects.

■ **A list broker** will act on your behalf to find you the best list, and can give you advice on selections, expected response rates and so on.

■ **Compilers** will build a list from scratch from your specifications – often commissioned by your list broker – taken from other lists.

If you want to find a good list broker, you can acquire a list of recommended brokers, to be sure you are dealing with someone trustworthy. A list is published by the Direct Marketing Association UK (DMA), at Haymarket House, 1 Oxendon Street, London SW1Y 4EE (0171 321 2525).

The more closely you work with your list broker, discussing your products, your mailshot objectives, the look of the intended mailing and so on, the better results they will be able to give you. They can commission a list compiler, who can produce a customized list with as much detail as you are prepared to pay for. They can even tell you that consumers who live on one side of a certain street are more likely to buy certain types of product through the post than consumers living on the opposite side of the street. Your list broker can help you decide how specific it is cost effective to make your list.

Buying in overseas mailing lists

This is a huge subject, and if you decide to build a database of overseas customers and prospects you would be well advised to use a good broker with experience of overseas lists. But it is worth bearing a few points in mind:

■ Just because a certain product appeals to a certain type of person in your own country, you cannot assume that it will appeal to the same type of person in another country. For example, lightweight briefcases might be popular with the under 40s in the UK, where older people might view them as being too modern. But in another country they might go down better with the over 50s. So don't simply aim to match your UK customer profile with a list of names from another country; research the market first.

■ International lists are usually drawn from subscribers to publications. You can acquire lists of people around the world, and you can choose what language publications they subscribe to, so you could be sure of mailing only English speakers, or only speakers of some other particular language.

■ National lists are local to individual countries and therefore work much in the same way as UK lists. You may need to go through a broker in the relevant country to find the best list.

■ Compiled lists for overseas names get a low response rate, and are best left alone unless they present the only way of creating a list. They are best for mailing small numbers of people, for example only businesses in a certain city where you will be attending an exhibition.

Market research

If the information you hold on each customer and prospect on your database is not as comprehensive as it might be, you will need to do some research to expand the data. The way to do this type of research is to send out a questionnaire to the people on your database asking for the additional information. The main stages in market research of this kind are:

■ identifying what you want to know;

■ deciding how you will find it out;

- designing a questionnaire;

- conducting the survey.

What do you want to know?

Have a look at the last chapter for ideas about the usual type of information that a direct marketing database would contain. You probably also have a fairly clear idea of the kind of information that might be helpful; you'll know that your product is likely to appeal more to some age groups or income brackets than others, or more to people who live in certain types of houses.

Collecting this information will not only tell you which prospects fit into which categories, it will also help you to build a fuller profile of your customers. This, in turn, will help you to target new customers. You might guess that your lightweight briefcase will appeal more to one age range than another, for example, but not be sure which age range exactly it will appeal to most. Establishing this will help you to target future campaigns better. If it is most popular with 20 to 29 year olds, it might be worth targeting university and college leavers. But if it goes down better with 30 to 39 year olds, universities might not be such a profitable target; graduate home-owners might be a better bet.

How will you establish the information?

If you are on a very tight budget, or surveying only a small number of customers, or finding out only a limited amount of data, you might want to undertake the research yourself. But for a survey of any size it is generally better to use a research agency. They will have the expertise to design the questionnaire clearly and suitably, and they will remove a huge amount of work from your shoulders, especially in analysing the data when it is returned.

An agency will need to be given a thorough brief if you want them to do the job properly. They will also need:

- a good background to the research – what data you hold at present, what more you need to know, and why;

- a clear objective;

- a budget;

- a time-scale to work to;

■   agreement with you about what response rate you expect to the survey.

The questionnaire

Even if you are using an agency to do your research, it is still useful to have a fairly good idea of what a good questionnaire ought to look like. It is very important that the questionnaire should be clear and easy to answer, or people simply won't bother. If questions are too personal people may not answer them, or they may answer them untruthfully. So the questionnaire must be carefully designed.

Remember that you are soliciting information to add to your database. So the answers must come back in a form in which they can be entered onto the database. It's no good asking open-ended questions such as 'What are your hobbies?' if you have 25 set codes you have to fit each answer into. What if someone puts down 'body piercing' and it doesn't fit any of the 25 choices? You'll have to list the 25 categories and ask people to tick those that apply to them.

Your questionnaire will ask the questions which your database asks you, but you will need to explain to the people you are surveying why it is that you want this information. Some of it may seem quite personal to some respondents, and these questions – such as asking what their income is – are best asked towards the end of the questionnaire. Include a covering letter which explains that you will be able to offer the respondent a better service in future if you know more about them.

If you only want to complete the details for a smaller number of names on your database you could conduct your questionnaire personally by phone. In this case the same principles apply, along with one or two others:

■   Explain why you are calling and how this information will benefit the customer or prospect.

■   Let them know how long the interview will take and ask whether now is a good time to call, or whether you can make an appointment to call later.

■   Ask the more personal questions towards the end of the interview.

■   Don't offer them a range of answers if they can answer in one or two words. Don't ask their age by saying 'Are you aged under 18, 18 to 25, 26 to 40, 41 to 55, 56 to 65 or over 65?' Simply ask them 'How old are you?' With something like a list of hobbies, say 'I'll read out a list of interests and activities. Please say 'yes' to any that you take part in.'

Conducting the survey

You want to achieve the highest response rate possible to this questionnaire, and there are certain things which will help you to do this:

■   You will get a better response from the people you have most contact with, and more from customers than prospects.

■   A covering letter explaining your objectives and the benefit to the respondent will increase the response.

■   An incentive for answering – for example, a discount, entry into a prize draw, a free gift – will boost the response.

■   A personalized letter will get a better response than a 'Dear Sir/ Madam' or 'Dear Customer' letter.

■   A reply-paid envelope will help.

■   Send out a reminder letter after 10 days or two weeks, with a further copy of the questionnaire, to those people who haven't replied.

■   Send out questionnaires to businesses on a Monday so they don't arrive at the end of the week, when they are more likely to go in the bin.

■   Send out questionnaires to consumers on a Thursday so that they arrive in time to be completed over the weekend.

Using your database for analysis

Your database software should allow you to analyse your customers' behaviour simply and easily whenever you want to. If you don't know how existing customers and prospects behave, how can you predict their future behaviour? The scope for analysis is almost limitless, and you will need to decide how best to find out what you want to know. Here are three examples to give you an idea.

EXAMPLE 1

Information needed: We mailed out two catalogues last month to see which was the most effective. We mailed half to prospects and customers in the top half of the alphabet and the other to people in the bottom half of the alphabet, to make the test as random as possible. Both catalogues generated a roughly equal response. Does this mean it doesn't matter which we mail out in future?

Analysis: We need to look at who responded to each catalogue. Let's analyse the respondents according to various criteria:

- Were they customers or prospects?

- Did they respond with an enquiry or an order?

- What was the average value of orders generated by each catalogue?

- How long had the respondents been receiving mailings from us?

- Where were the respondents located?

We may find that one catalogue attracts prospects more, while the other is more appealing to existing customers. One might generate more orders than the other, or generate higher value orders. It could be that one catalogue gets a better response than the other from new prospects, in which case it could be worth checking that the other isn't laid out in a way that confuses people who are not acquainted with the products.

This analysis could reveal that the two catalogues are nothing like as similar as it first seemed in the responses they generate. Perhaps one should be used in future for people who live in urban areas and the other for those in rural areas, or one for existing customers and the other for new propsects. Or perhaps, when you look at the average order value generated by each, one catalogue outstrips the other and should be used all the time in future. Database analysis is essential for answering this kind of question.

EXAMPLE 2

Information needed: We recently took a stand at a business-to-business exhibition. We sent free tickets to all our customers within a 50 mile radius, and about five per cent of them turned up at the stand. The mailing costs were quite high, and we want to know how to reduce them for future exhibitions by mailing only those people who are likely to turn up.

Analysis: We made a note of everyone who visited the stand, so we now need to analyse them to find out whether they fall into repeatable categories which we can limit our mailings to in future.

■   What postcode areas did they come from? This can be plotted as a graph to show how many people came from each area. This can be viewed against a map showing how far each postcode area is from the exhibition venue, to tell us how far people travelled to visit us. It may be that 50 miles is too far, and we only need mail people within a 25 or 30 mile radius in future.

■   How often and how recently have they ordered from us? Perhaps only our regular customers visit us – or maybe only those who don't know our products very well.

■   How much do they spend on an average order? Is it the big spenders who visit, or the smaller customers?

■   Which representative of the customer's company visits? Is it the managing director or one of the sales assistants? Is it the person who makes the buying decisions or someone further down the organization? If it varies, are there any useful correlations? Is it the buyer from smaller companies and someone more junior from larger companies?

■   What is the follow up like? Does the visit to the stand generate further appointments or orders from some customers and not others? If so, is there a pattern to it? Is it the less regular customers who follow the exhibition with a subsequent contact, or is it the top customers?

EXAMPLE 2 CONTINUED.

This sort of information should be easily accessible from a good database, and should help to make sure that we only invite those customers most likely to turn up – and follow the visit with subsequent contacts – in future.

EXAMPLE 3

Information needed: We have a broad range of products, which we tend to market all together. We think it would be cost effective to market some of these products individually to those people most likely to buy them, but we need to know who those people are.

Analysis: We need to draw up a profile of the people who currently buy each of these particular products, so that we can target people in future who match this profile.

■   What type of house or flat do they live in?

■   Which part of the country do they live in?

■   What age are they?

■   What type of jobs do they have?

■   What is their income bracket?

■   Do they buy other products from us as well? Which ones?

■   Do they order from us more or less frequently than average?

These kinds of questions will give us a picture of our typical customer for each product.

Using your database for selection

Every time you want to run a mailshot or telephone campaign, you will need to select the people you will be phoning or mailing. Sometimes you will want to contact all your customers, all your prospects or both, but often it will be more effective to contact only a section of them. For example, if you attend an exhibition you might want to invite customers based in the area only. The example earlier showed how analysis can help you identify which of these people are most likely to attend, so you can keep the cost of inviting customers as low as possible. This is a good example of how analysis and selection often go hand in hand; the analysis leads to the next selection.

Perhaps you want to mail a special offer only to those customers who have spent more than a certain amount with you over the last year, or you want to send details of your combined fax/photocopier/answerphone only to people who work from home. Maybe you want to target people in a certain age range, or contact only those who are both under 24 *and* drive a car.

A good database enables you to do all of this, and analysis and selection are the two crucial processes which your database must be able to perform. With a good database, the possibilities are limited only by your imagination. If you can think of a promising niche market, you should be able to analyse its potential and then select suitable customers and prospects.

Your marketing strategy

Once you have a versatile and well-maintained database, you can do any-thing. But you need to do it in the right way. When you are planning a campaign you need to go through the process in the right order. There are three key stages (see Box 2.1).

Your database is your company's equivalent of your personal Filofax. The business is bereft without it, and unable to function properly. It takes time to build it up but once it's there, it is indispensible. Use it well and keep it up to date and it will be your most valuable direct marketing asset. Fail to use it properly and you are wasting a golden opportunity.

BOX 2.1 PLANNING A CAMPAIGN

- First, decide which market you are targeting, and with what products or services. Is this campaign aimed at reaching new consumers with your catalogue? Selling your new range of products to existing business customers? Persuading prospects who have not yet bought to visit your showroom for a demonstration? If you think you know what needs doing, database analysis will confirm its potential, and the database will help you select the best people to approach.

- Next, decide on the most suitable way to approach the customers and prospects. Should you mail them or phone them? Or should you advertise? Or drop leaflets through their doors? (The chapters on each approach later on will enable you to choose the best medium each time.) Analysis of past campaigns should help you to answer this question.

- Finally, work out the creative aspects of the campaign. Should you be making any offers? What should the advertisement, mailshot, catalogue or leaflet look like? What should it say? If you have run this kind of campaign in the past, you can analyse the responses to see what works best with which customers. Perhaps certain products don't sell any better if you offer a discount than if you don't. Or certain types of customer respond better to glossy full colour brochures than to those printed in only one or two colours. Or you may always get the best response from business customers if you phone them first thing in the morning.

The Creative Dimension

The Creative Dimension

■   Many of the more creative skills of direct marketing apply to most or all branches of it – direct mail, mail order, door-to-door and so on. So it makes sense to discuss these umbrella skills first, before going on to see how to apply them to the individual direct marketing disciplines. In this chapter we will look at:

■   How to project the right image in everything you do.

■   Visual presentation.

■   Writing persuasive copy.

■   Using incentives.

These skills between them make up the creative element in direct marketing, and the creative side of marketing is often the aspect that puts you ahead of the competition. Even if the product is unique, you still need good creative skills to persuade your customers and prospects of its value to them.   ■

Many people think that creativity is a talent or a gift rather than a learnable skill. But this isn't true. It may come more naturally to some people than to others, and some lucky people have an ability to come up with ideas very easily, but the bulk of the creative input is simply a matter of skill and we can all learn it. Once you understand the principles you may not come up with all of the best ideas all of the time, but you'll be able to produce more than enough ideas that are more than sufficient to do the job.

The right image

Have you ever come across organizations which you find obstructive to deal with? Or penny-pinching – they'll have a row with you rather than give you a refund on damaged goods? Or organizations which are just plain rude? We all deal with this kind of company from time to time, although we usually avoid having to deal with them again if we can help it.

Some companies, on the other hand, are extremely friendly. Or they are particularly helpful, going out of their way to make your life easier. Or they're particularly reliable – and if things do go wrong you know you can trust them to put them right quickly and without any fuss.

Actually, the organizations we all deal with are none of these things. It is the people who work for them who exhibit these characteristics. But we associate these human personality traits with the organization itself. If you call up a company on the phone and the person you speak to is rude and unhelpful, you'll probably think 'I'm not calling there again; what an unpleasant company to deal with.' Never mind that their other 25 telephone answerers might be friendly and pleasant; you've tarred the whole organization with the same brush as the one person you spoke to.

Are you sure no one ever has this experience with your organization? Direct marketing is all about dealing directly with our customers, and that leaves us particularly exposed to being judged by them. If you never deal with a company directly, you will be far more likely to judge it kindly.

The importance of image

When you buy a branded product in a shop, you don't judge the manufacturer by the impression you have of the shop itself. Have you ever dealt directly with Colmans? No, you just buy their mustard from other people's shops. What about Heinz? Black & Decker? International Thomson Publishing (who publish this book)? Your image of all these companies is almost certainly determined by the product alone. If you like Heinz tomato ketchup, you'll assume their mayonnaise is good too. If you like this book, you'll be more likely to buy another book from International Thomson.

But when your customers buy from you, they judge you on far more than the product alone. They will judge you on the type of printed material you produce, on the attitude of your staff, and on the quality of the service you give. So it all has to be absolutely right. Image is a huge part of what makes people decide whether to do business with you or not. It makes the difference between buying from you and buying from your competitors.

Choosing your image

The image that you project will rub off on your product; everything is linked. The car you drive influences people's image of you, the way your friends decorate their houses affects your image of them, the kind of education your employees had contributes to the way you see them. In the same way, you cannot keep your product separate from your corporate image.

If people like your products, they will be inclined to like your organization; make sure you capitalize on this rather than undermining it. If you project a high quality, slightly formal image, people will expect your product to be high quality. If they think your organization is slightly downmarket and inclined to cut corners, they won't be too disappointed if the products they buy from you break after the first few times they use them. But if they see you as an upmarket organization with an emphasis on doing things properly, they will be upset if your product doesn't live up to this image – even if the price is exactly the same.

So you need to choose an image for yourself which suits your product – or you need to change your product if you think you could do more business with a product that projects a different image. In any case, your products, your printed materials, your telephone manner, your delivery vehicles, your packaging, your personal presentation and your customer service must all come into line with one another. If you send out different image messages, your customers and prospects are likely to judge you by the one you least want them to.

If you sell stainless steel kitchen equipment with a clean, shiny, hygienic image, and your customers see one of your delivery vehicles driving around splattered in mud and overdue for a fresh lick of paint, they will think 'Ugh! How can their products be sparkling clean when their vans are so disgusting?' Every aspect of your relationship with your customers and prospects must reflect the same image.

Everyone's best image

So what image should it reflect? Well, that depends on your organization and your products. But there are a few obvious aspects of image that all businesses would do well to project. Everyone would rather deal with businesses which are friendly and helpful. As we've already seen, one bad phone call or letter can turn a customer into an ex-customer, or a prospect into a never-going-to-be customer. So *all* your staff should be well trained in good customer handling.

Personal contacts are the most important of all when it comes to projecting an image. If someone receives a badly printed brochure from you and then speaks to a friendly, helpful member of staff, their image of your company will be generally good. Whereas if you send them a beautifully presented brochure and then they speak to a rude, obstructive person, they will quickly develop a very negative attitude towards you.

Direct marketing is all about making each customer feel that they have an individual relationship with you, so you must treat them all as individuals. Be as flexible as you can if they have special requests. If they want an order to be delivered to their daughter's address on the exact day of her birthday, do everything you can to arrange it. You might have to charge a premium, but send it by courier, or hold the order back for a few days, or process it manually for once (and add the details to the database later).

Have a system that allows for as much flexibility as possible, so that your customers each feel they are important enough to do things a little bit differently for. It's well worth it to keep their loyalty, and they really won't ask you to be flexible very often, unless your system needs improving. If your standard delivery time is 60 days you might get a lot of requests for faster delivery – but that should simply tell you to speed up your standard delivery time. A lot of similar requests for special treatment are usually a good indicator that your standard system isn't as helpful to your customers as it ought to be.

The best image for you

Apart from friendly and helpful service, which should be universal, you can create an image that is tailored to your organization and product range. The way to do this is to find two or three key words to describe your business, and make sure that everything you do suits this description.

Draw up a list of about half a dozen positive words which describe your organization, and another half dozen which describe your product. You're not looking for words you would like to describe the business, but words which accurately reflect it (which you hope will be much the same thing, but may not be). You're after adjectives describing a personality, the sort of words you might use to describe a person, not abstract nouns such as 'quality' or 'reliability'. If you have a broad range of products, think of words which describe the whole range. To get an objective view, ask other people to contribute – colleagues, other employees, customers and suppliers. Here is an idea of the kind of words you might use in each of your two lists:

■ extrovert	■ respectful	■ intelligent
■ ambitious	■ efficient	■ quiet
■ kind	■ fresh	■ smart
■ perfectionist	■ enthusiastic	■ easy going
■ traditional	■ organized	■ welcoming
■ elegant	■ ambitious	■ caring
■ hardworking	■ dynamic	■ professional
■ honest	■ innovative	■ humorous

You will probably have more than half a dozen words on each list, especially if you've managed to find plenty of people to help you come up with them. So reduce each list to the words that come up frequently – not necessarily the precise words – if one list contains the words 'business like' and the other one includes the word 'efficient' you are obviously dealing with the same kind of image. You may not have exactly half a dozen words on each list, but aim for between four and seven.

Now look at the overlap between the two lists. If there is no overlap – which is unlikely – it suggests that your product image and your organization image don't match each other at all. If this is the case, you need to make changes to bring them into line with each other. Your customers need to be able to judge your product by your organization's image and vice versa. Otherwise they will be confused and unsure of what to expect, which will deter them from doing business with you.

Assuming there is an overlap between the two lists, which is almost always the case, these overlap words are those which best describe your business's image as a whole. Hopefully you will have two or three words on this list; enough to give a rounded picture but few enough to project an uncluttered image.

Projecting your image

This is not only an interesting exercise to go through; it is an important process in presenting a clear, workable and positive image of your organization to your customers and prospects. You now need to make sure that everyone in your organization who ever deals with customers knows that these are the two or three words which best describe the image that your customers should receive whenever they deal with your company.

This does not mean that everyone has to suppress their own personality and pretend to be this imaginary person instead; real personalities have more dimensions than this. You are asking people to bring these aspects of their own personalities to the fore when they deal with customers. We are all capable of being either more extrovert or respectful or easy going or professional; the idea is to bring out the aspect which coincides with the corporate image.

Print these two or three image words on cards and pin them up by people's phones or on the office wall, so people remember what kind of impression they want to give to customers and prospects. And refer to them every time you plan a direct marketing campaign. Make sure that all the printed material, the phone calls, the packaging, the order fulfilment, the complaint handling and everything else reflects this image, as well as being friendly and helpful at every stage.

Visual presentation

A lot of direct marketing involves communicating with people through the visual medium: brochures, letters, catalogues, packaging, advertisements and so on. Some of these carry their own individual rules of good presentation which we will look at in the relevant chapters later on, but there are a number of important general guidelines for all creative materials which are worth examining now.

If you communicate with someone in writing, they will judge you by the visual impact of the material you send them before they ever read what you've written. Even if you've only written them a letter, they will form an opinion of your organization based on how well laid out it is, what your logo looks like, what colour it is and how long the letter is. You cannot help but be judged on your visual presentation, so you'd better get it right.

Colour

For some reason, different colours project different images. You may not be able to choose the colour of your logo, but you can control the colour of everything else. The most obvious example of image being projected through colour is the use of fluorescent colours. Can you imagine trying to sell expensive gentlemen's suits with a brochure printed in dayglo orange? At the other end of the scale, you wouldn't want to sell cheap and cheerful air fresheners and furry dice for cars using deep burgundy ink on parchment coloured paper – it just reeks of Victorian studies and expensive high quality goods. People would assume your products would cost them more than they wanted to pay.

You need to choose a colour which suits the image you want to put across. Here is a guide to some of the most commonly used colours and the impression they can give, but use your own common sense as well; subtle changes in colour can affect the image considerably. Dark sea green is a very traditional, high quality colour, while dark grass green is the colour typically used by conservation and nature organizations. See which colours match most closely with the image words you've chosen for your business.

- Red: dynamic;

- Pale blue: soothing;

- Dark blue: elegant;

- Yellow: cheerful;

- Green: sensible;

- Orange: down-to-earth and fun;

- Purple: unconventional and fun;

- Grey: modern but reserved;

- Brown and green together: rustic and homespun;

- Deep, rich colours such as burgundy, midnight blue and deep green: traditional and perhaps a little old-fashioned;

- Pastel shades: feminine and delicate;

- Contrasting colours: up-to-date;

- Complementary colours: traditional;

- Soft, earthy colours: peaceful and honest.

You can combine colours, but if the colours you choose send out very different messages you risk confusing your audience. Orange and deep burgundy, for example, would send out a very mixed message. But it can be very effective to use colours whose messages complement each other. For example, you might be selling a product with a traditional image but a modern spin to it – perhaps fountain pens which write upside-down. You could use a very traditional colour, for example a deep midnight blue, and then add a flash of something very modern and hi-tech, such as silver.

Paper

The paper or card that you print on is also very important to the image you project. Thin, highly glossed paper looks cheaper than thicker paper with a softer sheen. Flimsy plain paper for letters looks less impressive than a heavier laid paper (laid paper is that type often used for letters which is covered in tiny ridges).

There's no absolute right or wrong. You might want to give a simple, inexpensive image, so the classier papers might not be suitable for your business – they might make your product seem too expensive or valuable for what the customer needs.

Layout

Once again, the way you put the design onto the page, in an advertisement, a letter, a brochure or anything else, says a lot about your organization. If you cram lots of information on, it suggests a cheap and cheerful image. This may be exactly what you need, but beware of confusing the reader's eye, or they may not bother to work out what you're saying.

The more space you leave – 'white space', your designer may call it – the more elegant the page will appear and the easier to read it will be. A clean, uncluttered look is often the best since it is easy on the eye.

Whether you go for a busy, dynamic image or a clean simple image, you need to make sure that the overall look of the page is aesthetically pleasant and balanced. You are usually better off having a professional designer design your material, but you can use desktop publishing software and design it yourself. However, make sure that it is being designed by someone with a really good eye for design, not just someone who understands how to use the software package. And then make sure that they design it in the style that sends out the right message, not just in a way that they think looks pretty.

If the most important thing you want your readers to see is the photographs – if that is what will sell your product – put them in the dominant position on the page. If the text is your most important feature, make it clear and put it where it will attract the eye. Don't use clever but unreadable devices such as printing in white on a black background, or using so many columns that each line can only fit two or three words, or printing in a fancy typeface, in huge or tiny letters, or in capitals. If you want people to read the text, don't get too clever. Just give them nice, simple text like they're used to reading.

General presentation

You need to keep people's interest, so you want plenty of visual stimulation. One well-chosen photograph might achieve this, or it may take more. But people like looking at pictures, so make sure each page (except in a letter) has an illustration, photograph, chart, diagram, table, line drawing or something to catch people's interest. Just don't let the page get so busy that they can't tell what they are supposed to be looking at.

People look at a page or an advertisement in a particular order:

1   First, they look at the headline.

2   If that grabs their attention, they will look at the illustrations.

3   Next they look at the captions.

4   After that they will read the text, scanning from the top left hand corner to the bottom right, picking out the subheadings if there are any.

Of course, you won't necessarily have all these features in a letter or a mail order catalogue, and we'll look at the details later on in the relevant chapters, but this is a general principle that you can adapt for the specific material you are designing.

Writing persuasive copy

There are special formulae for writing headlines, advertisements and direct mail letters, which we will look at later. But there are also general rules for creative copy writing which apply whatever kind of material you are producing, and we'll look at these now.

Who are you writing this for?

You need to have a very clear idea of who this letter, advertisement, brochure or catalogue is intended for, because the way you write it will be determined by this. Suppose you are selling fountain pens which write upside-down. Are you selling them to university students? Or to retired solicitors? Or to senior managers in computer and media organizations?

You will need to adopt a different style and draw attention to different features of the pen depending on who you are talking to. You would use a different vocabulary to talk to undergraduates from the one you would use for retired solicitors. One of the beauties of direct marketing is that you can communicate with all three of these groups – and any others you want to target – and you can treat them all separately. Write three different sets of material and send them out in three separate mailings.

But for each piece of material you write, you must know who it is aimed at. The best way to do this is to create an imaginary person (perhaps based on a real one whom you happen to know) and keep a clear picture of them in your head, and imagine you are writing to them individually. This should also give the material the personal touch that will make each customer or prospect who sees it feel important. You might have a friend whose son or daughter just fits the bill as your imaginary student, or an ageing godparent who is a perfect model for your retired solicitor – it always helps to base your imaginary reader on a real person, but it certainly isn't essential.

What are you trying to achieve?

The next thing to establish, before you actually begin to write, is what the aim of the exercise is. You want the reader to contact you as a result of reading this ad, letter or brochure – that's what direct marketing is about. But you might not expect them to place an order immediately. If this is a mail order catalogue, you probably do. But if it is an ad, you might be asking them to pick up the phone, or cut out the coupon. If it's a letter or a brochure you might be hoping they'll make an appointment, or send for a free trial pack.

This might sound obvious – it should sound obvious – but a lot of people don't consciously identify their objective when they write marketing material, and the result can be an unfocused piece of writing which leaves the reader confused about what they are supposed to do next.

It's no good being unrealistic. There are some things you can't hope to sell from an ad in the paper. People will want to see pictures and diagrams, and have more information than you can fit in an ad. For example, few people would buy an expensive climbing frame for their kids on the basis of a small display ad at the back a magazine. They will want to send off for several brochures to compare your product with your competitors' versions, look at detailed photographs, find out how long they take to assemble, decide which modules they want and so on. Your aim should be to persuade them to phone you for a brochure, not to ring and place an order.

What's more, if people contact you for information only, you can add them to your database as 'warm prospects', so you can contact them in future if they don't buy in response to the brochure. If the letter or advertisement asked for an order, many of these people would never have contacted you at all if they weren't sure they wanted to buy, and then you wouldn't know who they were. Asking for less than an actual order is often the best way to find out who your best prospects are.

Benefits not features

People don't want to know what your product can do, they want to know what it can do *for them*. When you write about your product, you must write about its benefits for the person who you are writing to, not simply about its features. Let me give you an example. Your fountain pen writes upside-down. That is its key feature. But that is of no use in itself; it is the application of that feature which brings a benefit, and you must spell out the benefit for your readers. Don't assume that they will work it out for themselves.

The benefit is that since the pen writes at any angle, you can use it in situations where you can't normally use a fountain pen. What situations? Well, that depends on the reader. If you're writing for designers, tell them they can use it when they're writing on a drawing board. If this is a brochure for retired professionals, tell them the pen is perfect for doing the crossword on the train. If you're advertising to students, tell them it's ideal for writing standing up or lying down.

Always look at the product from the customers' point of view, and think about what it can do for them – what benefit it will bring them – and then spell this out in the material you're writing.

Writing plain English

The very first thing you should do when you sit down to write is to decide what you want to say, and in what order. Never mind for the moment how you're going to say it. In some cases there is a formula to follow (as we'll see in later chapters), but in any case you should start by deciding what goes into each section of the formula.

What you'll need to do initially is to rough out the brochure, ad or letter with a kind of heading for each paragraph. Use any kind of note form that suits you, but give yourself a skeleton format to work to. Here's an example:

1 Hello.

2 Intro to product.

3 Benefits to reader.

4 What to do if you're interested.

5 Polite goodbye.

The point of this exercise is to give you a checklist to make sure you've missed nothing out, a prompt sheet while you're writing, and a waffle-guard. By that I mean that you're less likely to start waffling (which some people are very prone to when they write) if you have written yourself a plan for each paragraph.

Once you start to flesh out this skeleton, there are a few simple rules to follow to make sure that your writing is straightforward and easy to read.

Use the second person

Always address the reader as you. Don't say 'Our customers will find our fountain pens extremely useful', say 'You will find our fountain pens extremely useful.' (If you're writing for a younger audience you can elide the first two words and say 'You'll find . . .'.)

Using the second person is more friendly, and it makes the reader feel that you are talking to them individually; that you know who they are. If you don't use the second person, the material will read like some kind of form letter, and the reader will feel uninvolved. By the same token, refer to your own organization as 'we', not 'the manufacturers' or 'the company'.

Avoid jargon

'Jargon' can be hard to define, because what is jargon to me might be everyday language to you. But even if you can't define it, it is simple to identify. It doesn't matter how used you are to a certain word; what matters is whether your readers are familiar with it. If all your readers are specialist engineers, say, who know your industry better than you do, you can use words that would leave the likes of me completely baffled. 'Tolerance' means something completely different to a technical person from what it means to the rest of us. So if your readers are not all experts in the field, you will have to simplify your language.

Suppose you sell computer hardware. If you sell it to computer managers in large organizations, you can use specialist language. But if you are writing for people buying a PC for home use, they may not know what a VDU is; better to call it a screen – they'll understand that. So suit your vocabulary to your readers, and don't use words that they would regard as jargon.

Use short words, sentences and paragraphs

People find short words and sentences easier to understand. That doesn't mean that they don't know any big words. It means that if you give them a page of long words and sentences to read, they might think they have taken it all in, but a test will show that they can't answer many questions about the content. It just doesn't go in.

By the same token, long paragraphs are hard to take in. As soon as the reader looks at the size of the paragraph coming up, they are likely to feel their heart sink – often they simply won't bother to read it. Remember that for you, this mailing might be the most crucial business decision of your career, but to your target readers, it's just another bit of paper coming through the letterbox. They will think nothing of dropping it in the bin at any point if it seems like too much work to read or think about.

As a broad rule of thumb, try to make sure that when the paragraph is printed in the final version it is wider than it is deep, unless you are using narrow columns.

Use active verbs

Active verbs are doing verbs, passive verbs have things done to them. Active verbs give your writing a more dynamic feel. Say 'We will send the goods as soon as we get your order', not 'Your goods will be despatched as soon as your order is received.' Occasionally you will find that you need to use passive verbs, but limit them to one in every four or five sentences.

Use concrete nouns

'Delivery will be provided within 28 days' uses an abstract noun: delivery. These are harder for the reader to take in. It would be much better to say 'We will deliver within 28 days.' A lot of abstract nouns end with '-tion'; these are much better replaced with concrete nouns or verbs. You can replace the word 'transportation' with 'car', 'information' with 'leaflet', or 'correspondence' with 'letter'.

Making it look readable

We saw earlier that it is quite hard for the reader to take in long words, sentences and paragraphs. But you can do more for your readers than simply shorten these features. There are several ways to make the finished material look approachable and easy to read:

- Double or one-and-a-half space text so that there is less of it on each page, making it easier to read.

- Leave generous margins, again creating plenty of 'white space' and making the text look easy to manage.

- Use headings and subheadings to break up the text, and to act as signposts for the readers so they can find the information they want.

- Use lists with numbers or bullet points for information which can be presented this way, such as a list of examples of when an upside-down pen would be useful.

- Put information in boxes as self-contained little articles with their own heading: 'How does the pen work?'

Using incentives

By far the biggest danger with direct marketing is that your readers will think 'Hmm... interesting' and then do nothing. You can't even identify which of them were interested if they never reply. So how do you encourage them to respond? Incentives. Invite them to enter a prize draw, qualify for a free gift or have a discount. Incentives give you huge scope for creativity, but you have to think them through. There are two main considerations which will conflict if you aren't careful:

1   They must genuinely attract the reader to respond.

2   They must be cost effective for you.

There are three basic types of incentive you can offer:

1   prize schemes;

2   gifts;

3   discounts.

Each one of these has advantages and disadvantages, so we'll look at them each in turn.

Prize schemes

This is the least expensive scheme to run, and generally the most effective. However if you aren't careful there is a danger that it can have a down-market, mass appeal image which may not suit your business. There are two main types of prize scheme: draws and contests.

Draws are based entirely on chance. You offer readers tickets and if they return them, they will be entered in the draw. Alternatively you tell them that the draw has already taken place but you don't know who has won; the winning numbers have been allocated randomly by computer and you invite the reader to send in their numbers to be checked. It is illegal to make entry into a draw conditional on purchase of the product, but prize draws attract high order response rates because people believe that their chances will be better if they place an order at the same time.

Contests involve some kind of skill, from spot the ball to 'Describe in no more than 20 words how our upside-down fountain pen can make your life easier'. You will need to set up a panel of judges if you run a contest, and it is sensible to incorporate a tie-breaking task just in case the judges cannot choose between two or more entrants. You can make entry to a contest conditional on purchase, or restrict it to any other group. This can be very useful in persuading people to buy in order to qualify for the contest.

The most popular prizes for these schemes are, in order: cash, cars and holidays. It's worth offering a cash alternative to other prizes to encourage people who don't drive, for example, to enter. Offer runner-up prizes as well, since people believe that this increases their chances of winning. And encourage people to reply promptly, since giving them the opportunity to delay can slash your response rate. You could make certain prizes conditional on replying before a certain date.

Skimping on prizes is not worthwhile. If people don't perceive the prize to be worth substantially more than the value of their order, they won't bother to enter. You won't tempt many people with the offer of a bottle of champagne. If you can't run to the cost of a car at least offer a trip in a hot air balloon, or a year's free petrol. But you can often negotiate very good deals with prize suppliers in exchange for the good publicity you are giving them.

Promoting your incentive

People are naturally suspicious. You must make sure that your offer seems plausible, especially if you are running a prize scheme of some kind, otherwise people will suspect some kind of a con. They will think that the draw may be rigged, or that there aren't really any prizes at all. You should contact a marketing lawyer for advice on printing terms and conditions, and making sure you comply with the law, but you also need to convince your readers.

The most important thing is the ticket or voucher that your reader has to return to you in order to enter the draw or contest. This should look as serious and important as possible, in order to persuade them that you are running a serious competition.

You also need to pay attention to the copy you write to persuade people to enter the scheme. Most importantly, you have to convince them that there is a realistic chance of winning a prize. Tell them how they were selected, and explain what will happen if they win – when and how the prize will be presented. Describe how it feels to drive the car or sit on the beach in the Canaries. Encourage them to dream.

And you must also add to the credibility of the overall scheme – persuade the reader that you are reliable and honest. You can do this by writing about previous winners in past draws or contests, the identities of the judges, and the value of the prizes.

Gifts

The disadvantage of offering a free gift with every order is that you have to give it to everyone – including all the people who were going to place an order anyway. On the other hand, a good offer can do a lot to boost your order response rate. Good free gift offers tend to have certain features in common:

- They appeal to just about every customer.

- They feel valuable, not tacky and cheap.

- They are unusual.

- They are relevant to the product, or even enhance it (a free holder or protective cover, for example).

- They are photogenic so you can persuade people easily that they want the gift.

You could offer a smart, wooden-handled gardening knife with the customer's initials on the handle, as an incentive to subscribe to a gardening magazine. Or you could offer a leather-cornered desk blotter with your range of office furniture.

You can also use gifts as thank you presents for long term or high value customers, to increase their loyalty. If you do this, you must make sure the gift is not an insult to their loyalty. If your budget is limited, better to give a valuable gift to your top 500 customers than a cheap one to the top 5000 customers.

Discounts

Discounts have an obvious cash value, and are therefore often more popular than gifts. However, they share the disadvantage that you have to give the discount to everyone. On the other hand, with a good database you can restrict the offer to first time buyers or good customers, or any other group you wish.

When it comes to offering incentives to business customers, discounts don't work very well if they save money for the customer's company rather than for the customers themselves. This is why most petrol companies offer vouchers to collect and exchange for gifts; so much petrol is paid for by drivers' employers that a discount would fail to attract an awful lot of drivers. Airlines offering free air miles operate on the same principle.

Summary

The creative side of direct marketing really isn't that difficult. Give the right impression in everything you do, create a good visual impression every time you advertise or mail your prospects and customers, write plain, clear English, and give a good incentive to encourage people to respond.

You will find that as time goes on you become more practised at coming up with good free gifts and offers, but you're not looking for wild and wacky ideas, just something that will appeal to your readers. And if you can learn to look at your products from *their* point of view, that shouldn't be too demanding a challenge.

Direct Response Advertising

■ You can run an advertising campaign that is intended simply to raise awareness of your product, service or organization – such as 'Go to work on an egg'. But direct response advertisements are different. They ask the customer or prospect to take action: send back the coupon, pick up the phone, ask for a free sample, visit the showroom, arrange an appointment or make some other form of contact.

There are three main places where you can place your ad, and we'll look at each of them in turn:

■ press;

■ television;

■ radio.

But wherever you advertise, you will need to follow the same format for persuading your readers, viewers or listeners to respond. The standard format is generally known by its mnemonic AIDA, and we'll look at it in just a moment. ■

Is advertising the best approach?

Before you go ahead with advertising – or any other form of direct marketing – you must first establish whether it is the best way to reach your target audience. And to do this, you must be very clear about who your target audience is.

We've already seen how keeping a good database can help with this. You want to target your audience as precisely as possible. Once you have identified them, you will need to establish two things about your database:

1   How many of your target audience are included on your database?

2   What will it cost to reach them by any other means such as mail or phone?

If your target audience is 'people who have ordered from us in the last six months' they should all be on your database. However, suppose you sell library steps and ladders and you want to target 'people with large collections of books'. There are probably plenty of them who are not on your database. What's more, you may not have identified those of the people who *are* on your database who have large collections of books. So mailing or phoning are unlikely to be the best approaches to communicating with your target audience.

The next step is to cost out the options, and see what it would cost to buy in a mailing list, and how well targeted it would be. You might decide, for example, that people who buy expensive sets of encyclopaedias often have their own library of books (you may even be able to establish whether this is true or not – someone may have done some research). Would it be possible to buy in a mailing list from an encyclopaedia publisher of their recent customers? If so, what would be the cost?

You also need to find out the cost of advertising. Where would you advertise? Again, you want to target as well as possible, so you might want to use the *Times Literary Supplement*, or a specialist magazine about books. Or it might be better to insert a leaflet with someone else's mailshot – a book club for example. (Inserts are about four or five times more expensive than a full-page ad, but the response can be five or six times higher.)

So don't start by thinking 'Let's advertise.' Start by thinking 'Here's who we want to reach. What's the best way to do it?' Advertising is often the best answer, but not nearly so often as some people think.

AIDA

AIDA describes the four ingredients that every advertisement should include, in the order in which they should happen. It stands for:

- Attention;
- Interest;
- Desire;
- Action.

First, you need to attract the reader's, viewer's or listener's *attention*; then you must grab their *interest* to keep them there until they reach the end of the ad. Once you have their interest you must kindle their *desire* to own your product or use your service, and finally you must persuade them to do something about it – to take *action* – and you must tell them how.

You might well use an agency to design your ads for you, rather than doing it yourself, but even if you do it's worth knowing the principles of writing ads. It puts you in a better position to recognize whether your agency is showing you a promising design. And if your budget is tight, writing your own ads – especially press ads – can be very sensible.

Attention

Attention is almost always secured with an eyecatching headline or – in the case of radio – with an earcatching opening line. But unless your ad is very small it is often better to attract attention with an unusual or interesting picture.

People always scan written ads in the same order:

- the photograph or illustration and the headline, together;

- the caption;

- the bottom right hand corner (to see who is advertising).

This process takes about $1\frac{1}{2}$ seconds, and if you haven't attracted their attention by then, you've lost them. So work on the picture and the headline. The picture should be a photograph if possible; they are more believable than drawings, and people are always suspicious of ads, especially ads placed by companies they haven't heard of before.

Photographs

For a photograph to attract attention, it must be unusual in some way. Something the reader doesn't recognize, or something taken from an unusual angle, or showing someone doing something interesting, or a very beautiful or haunting picture. Or a picture which creates atmosphere. No one's attention will be grabbed by a picture of an ordinary object in ordinary surroundings doing nothing at all.

For your library steps you could create atmosphere by photographing elegant library steps in a beautiful old library with the shelves full of leather-bound books. Just about any book lover (your target readers) should be attracted by that. Or you could photograph a set of library steps which converts into a chair from an unusual angle, so as to make the reader wonder what it is and stop for a second look. Be wary of being too cryptic, mind you; the readers may simply give up on your ad before they've started.

One of the important things to bear in mind when you produce an ad is that the readers aren't nearly as interested in it as you are. Think about the newspapers and magazines you read, and the television you watch. Every ad has had money spent on it and has been placed by someone who cares whether you read or watch it or not. And do you? On average, only 20 per cent of readers will notice the headline of a small ad – and only one in eight of those will read any further. Slightly more people will notice the headline of a larger ad, but you still have to attract attention to get people to look any further.

Headlines

What should the headline say? It should draw attention to a benefit of the product (we looked at focusing on benefits rather than features in the last chapter). But which benefit? Well, every product should have a unique selling proposition, or USP. This term refers to something which makes your product different from everyone else's. Something that sets it apart from the competition.

In the case of the library chair that converts into steps, its versatility and its space-saving benefits are both USPs. A few other people make them, but the real competition is non-convertible steps and ladders. Library step/chairs are traditional, so they fit with the feel of a traditional library, but they are more compact. This is the USP you can use in your headline. You might say: *The traditional way to save on space but not on convenience.* If the photograph clearly shows a traditional library there is no need to use the word 'library' in the headline. If not, you could say: *The traditional way to save on space but not on convenience in your library.*

A USP doesn't have to be something no one else has. It could be something no one else has at the price. Or it could be part of the service rather than the product itself. You could give the best after-sales service, or the fastest delivery, or the widest range of colours, or the most reliable product at the price. You might be an optician who specializes in being good at providing eye tests and glasses for elderly people. You might have plenty of disabled facilities and wheelchair access, and offer cups of tea and suitable magazines for people waiting for prescriptions.

There are a few useful guidelines for writing headlines; all useful tips turned up from research into what makes people look at ads.

- Assuming you have the space without cramping the text, headlines with between 10 and 17 words are the most likely to be read.

- People are more likely to remember the headline if you include the price in it. However, this only applies if the price is appealing, and if your customers are price sensitive.

- Make your headline as specific as possible. Don't say *Save money with our special offer . . .* , say *Save £20 with our special offer . . . .*

- If headlines are too cryptic people won't bother trying to work them out.

- Headlines printed in capitals and lower case letters are much easier to read than headlines printed in all capitals.

■ Headlines are more likely to be read if they are placed above the main text, not in the middle of it or at the bottom.

■ A full stop at the end of a headline puts people off reading any further.

Captions

You don't have to use a caption, but since people who are still interested after the headline will read the caption next, it is another opportunity to persuade them to read the main body of the text if they were starting to waver. So it is a good idea – especially if there is quite a lot of text for them to pluck up the enthusiasm to read.

The caption should not simply state what the photograph is of, but should add to what you have already said, and increase the reader's interest. So you might say: *The two-in-one ladder chair is a copy of a design which was popular with the Victorians in the 19th century.* You've indicated broadly what the product is, and you've caught the imagination of people who want to reproduce an old-fashioned look in their libraries. But you should have left people feeling they want to read more about it.

Interest

Your next job, once you have the readers' attention, is to hold their interest long enough to get them to read right through the ad. And the best way to do that is to talk about the subject everyone likes to hear about best: themselves. Tell your readers about what your product can do for them; about the benefits to them of having it. Tell them how it's the simplest way to reach those books that are too high to get at easily . . . how elegant it will make their library look . . . how it will give them somewhere to sit and study their books once they've reached them down from the shelves, even in a corridor or room with very little space for furniture . . . and so on.

Don't begin the text by repeating what you said in the headline; that wouldn't be interesting enough. Tell them something new. And find other interesting things to tell them: *The library step chair was very popular with the Georgians, and the Victorians developed the range of designs . . .* Your regular research should tell you what your readers are most likely to be concerned about – which benefits will appeal to them most. Perhaps the elegant image to show off to their friends is very important; or perhaps they are more interested in saving space. It may depend on where you are advertising; a publication with an older readership might be more concerned about the fact that the steps are very stable and won't fall over.

Here are a few more ways to hold the readers' interest:

- **Ask questions**. Questions that require answers, rather than rhetorical questions, encourage people to keep reading. *Do you have difficulty reaching the books on the top shelves?* or *Would you like to expand your bookshelf space upwards, but don't know how you'd reach the books at the top?* or *How can you create an elegant, traditional library?*

- **Use pictures**. Photographs are more credible than line drawings, and for many products more useful. Show two photographs side by side, one of the step chair in its chair position, and one of it converted into steps. Or show someone in the process of converting it. People in photographs give a personal touch; they also add movement and activity visually, and they are often essential to give the reader an idea of scale. You might know that your sofa seats four people comfortably, but if you don't put four people in one of the photos the reader might think it looks like a two-seater sofa.

- **Repeat certain words**. Your writing will have a flow which encourages people to keep reading if you use the same word two or three times (a word you want to sink in): . . . *elegant to look at, elegant to use* . . .

- **Encourage the reader.** You can encourage the reader to keep reading from one paragraph to the next by starting each paragraph with a phrase which links it to the previous paragraph: *And another thing* . . . or *Not only that* . . . or *What's more* . . .

- **Humour**. Well-judged humour will make your readers warm to you, but humour which falls flat will turn them off. So use it if you're sure (test it out on plenty of friends, colleagues and anyone else you can think of first), but if in doubt, steer clear of it.

- **Personal recommendation**. Anything in quotes encourages people to read it, and testimonials from satisfied customers are one of the best ways to hold your readers' interest. The best way to get them is to write the testimonial yourself and then ask a satisfied customer if they would be happy for you to put their name to it. Tell them you've written it to save them time and effort; you could write three and let them choose the one they prefer. A testimonial with no name attached to it looks like a fake.

■ **Use subheadings**. Unless the text is very short, use subheadings. People will read these before they read the text itself, so make them interesting – use them to trail the benefit that is described in the next paragraphs: *Make using your library a real pleasure* or *Save valuable space* or *Somewhere to sit and read.*

■ **Keep the text together**. Don't break the text up with anything other than subheadings. If you interrupt it with illustrations, coupons, main headlines or anything else you will deter readers from reading beyond the interruption.

Desire

Just because someone is interested in the ad, it doesn't automatically mean that they want to buy the product. Kindling a desire for the product is not something that follows capturing the reader's interest; it runs alongside it.

If the reader is interested enough to read the ad, the likelihood is that they have some desire for the product or service. But they will often make excuses to themselves for not buying it. They will say to themselves 'I bet it's really expensive' or 'It's probably very rickety' or 'I expect it only comes in that dark wood in the photo, and it wouldn't look right in my library'. Your regular customer research should tell you what people's most common reservations about your product are. So answer them.

If you are on the phone, or face to face, your prospects can express their reservations and you can respond. But with an ad, they may never contact you if they are unsure about the product. So as the ad goes on, you should shift the emphasis from explaining the benefits to reassuring the reader about the worries that your research tells you they are likely to have. Don't refer to the potential worry; simply provide the answer: *It's two pieces of furniture for the price of one . . .* or *Following the classic Victorian design, it is both elegant and extremely stable* or *We make the library step chair in two designs and three different finishes.*

Action

Interest and desire are crucially important, of course, but they are worth nothing without action. Your reader must make some kind of contact as a result of reading your ad, and you will need to tell them what to do.

The best option is to provide a coupon for them to fill in and return. The reason for this is that more people both read and respond to ads which have coupons, and the bolder the coupon the better. Make sure it is in an easy place to cut out, preferably the outside corner of a page. But if you can, offer a phone number to call as well for those who can't be bothered to fill in the coupon, cut it out, find an envelope, address it, find a stamp . . . and so on. If you expect a large response, arrange a freephone or local-rate number with the telephone company so the reader doesn't have to fork out for the call.

There are other options as well as (or instead of) the coupon:

■ **Pick up the phone**. It's much friendlier if you can give people a name to ask for when they ring. If you expect a large response to the ad, make sure you have the staff to deal with it. Make it clear that people can phone for more information; they don't have to be ready to place an order before they call.

■ **Fax or e-mail**. Some people might find it easier to respond this way. It combines the speed of the phone with the official feeling of having something in writing. If you are producing a loose-leaf insert in someone else's mailing or magazine, rather than an ad printed on a newspaper or magazine page, you can easily include a fax reply form.

■ **Reply-paid card or freepost address**. Again, this saves people money and, if you insert an envelope for them, it also saves them having to write out the address.

■ **Form to fill out and return**. Order form, enquiry form, registration form, application form and so on.

Whichever of these options you use, make sure the reader knows what happens next. Will you send them an information pack? Phone them within a week? Deliver the product within 48 hours? Let them know what to expect, and tell them if there is a no-quibble money back guarantee (if you're asking for orders, this is a big help).

Press advertising

Before you decide to advertise in the press, you need to know why you are doing it. Press advertising is often relatively untargeted compared with other forms of direct marketing. You are likely to pay to reach a lot of people who will never be customers in order to reach those who are genuine prospects. However, press advertising certainly has its uses. There are four main reasons for direct advertising in the press:

1   **To generate sales**. Perhaps few people would buy an expensive set of library steps straight from the page without more information, but some products sell very well in response to ads. Saucepan sets, for example, seem to sell well this way.

2   **To find specialized prospects**. Sometimes it is almost impossible to find a list of the kind of prospects you are after. It may be, for example, that no one has ever drawn up a list of people who have their own libraries at home. So you can use a trade or specialist magazine or newspaper ad to persuade your prospects to identify themselves. You may have to advertise to a circulation of 50,000 in order to reach the 2000 who have libraries – not all of whom will respond – but it is still the most cost effective option if you cannot identify them otherwise.

3   **To generate a large volume of enquiries**. If you want to add names to your database, or generate enquiries which you can pursue by other means – post or phone for example – to convert into sales, press advertising can bring in high numbers of enquiries more cost effectively than other media such as direct mail.

4   **To perform two functions at once**. You might want to run an awareness advertising campaign to draw people's attention to your products generally – which isn't a form of direct marketing since it requires no specific response. But suppose you also want to run a direct response campaign of some kind. In this case, running a direct advertising campaign, rather than direct mail for example, will serve to raise awareness of your products with some readers while eliciting a direct response from others. Equally a direct response ad might generate both enquiries and sales. Or you could use it to generate both direct sales and retail support, for example by including a money-off coupon to use at your retail outlets. Where you have

more than one objective, press advertising can be the best way to achieve both cost effectively.

Where to advertise

There is a wide choice of press to advertise in, some more effective than others. You need to establish the number of people each publication reaches, and you also need to know the type of reader. You can establish this by talking to the staff at the publication, by looking at a copy of it, and by referring to directories such as BRAD (British Rate and Data). BRAD is produced monthly (you'll find the latest copy in your nearest main library), and it lists every publication – free and paid-for – in Britain, detailing advertising rates, circulation, advertising deadlines and so on. However, for a broad overview, here are the main types of publication you could advertise in:

- **Local papers**. These offer untargeted advertising. If your product has broad appeal, the local paper may well be the place to advertise, but only if you are a relatively local or regional organization. It is very expensive to advertise in a lot of local or regional papers – about three times as expensive per thousand circulation as the national press. If you do decide to advertise here, you want your ad to be on the most frequently read pages. In the case of the local papers, the pages people most often turn to are the announcements page and the problems page (if there is one), followed by the horoscope and then the letters page, and then the news pages. The pages designated for advertising are the ones least frequently read.

- **National press**. These papers may be expensive but if you want a broad coverage they can be very cost effective. The combined circulation of the 20-odd national UK papers is over a hundred million copies a week (averaging five to each household), so your ad is likely to be seen by a huge number of people.

- **Freesheets**. These are cheap to advertise in, but they often get a very low response – a lot of people put them straight in the bin when they come through the letterbox. The response rate is better for freesheets which don't come through the door but can be picked up at the local newsagent or post office – only the people who actually want to read them pick them up. Once again, however, you need a product with a very general appeal to be worth advertising here.

- **Trade and professional publications**. These are often the best places to advertise business-to-business products. They can be expensive to advertise in, but this is because they are well targeted – they are often sold only by subscription. On the other hand, it can sometimes be very easy and more cost effective to reach exactly the same people by direct mail.

- **General interest magazines**. If your products' appeal is fairly broad but not universal, this might be your best option. You can advertise in gardening magazines, computer magazines, car magazines and so on, which have a fairly broad catchment.

- **Specialist magazines**. If you look under the 'Literary' section of BRAD, it will tell you which publications are directed exclusively at book lovers, and you'll find some are about poetry, some are targeted at students, some are for people who want to write books themselves. These magazines have a smaller but more targeted circulation than general interest magazines, and can therefore be very useful.

- **Subscription magazines**. People who subscribe to magazines tend to be loyal readers. In fact, 60 per cent of magazine subscribers read over half the ads. Once again, you pay for the fact that you can expect a good response rate to a well designed ad in these publications.

The good news and the bad news

It's worth looking at a quick run down of the pros and cons of press advertising, as a final checklist to be sure that it is the best medium for you each time. On the plus side:

- The production costs are low.

- The campaign is fairly simple and fast to organize, compared with orchestrating a direct mail or telephone campaign, for example.

- There are relatively few variables – you can estimate the cost very accurately when budgeting, and the publishers can give you reliable indications of circulations, readerships and so on.

- You can reach just about anyone so long as you pick the right publication, or the right mix of publications.

- It is easy to test. Run the same ad in two different publications to find out which is the most effective. Or run two different ads in the same publication to see which gives you the highest response. Or run the ad regionally to begin with. Or the same ad on different days of the week – there are plenty of ways to find out how to get the best response before you launch into the full scale campaign.

And on the downside:

- The space in a press ad is limited compared with direct mail (although it is better for the 'action' details, such as a coupon, than TV or radio ads).

- There is less scope for creativity than there is with direct mail.

- Unless your product's appeal is very broad, regional and local press advertising tend to be expensive compared with other media.

When and how to advertise in the press

You will find that all those ad sales staff are telling you the truth when they say that it is more effective to advertise several times in a row than only once. Eventually the response is likely to fall off, and you'll find out from experience when that happens with your own product. However, there are a few rules of thumb:

- The smaller the ad, the longer you will go on getting a response from repeating it.

- The more interesting or unusual a product, the longer you can run the ad.

- The larger the circulation of the publication, the longer the ad can run.

- In general, direct response ads are subject to the law of diminishing returns and will eventually fall off. If you want to repeat the series of ads after a break, you will need to test the response to find out how long a break between advertising campaigns works for your own product.

Size is important. The response to an ad is generally in direct response to its size. So a half page ad will generate 50 per cent of the response that a full page ad in the same publication will generate. Since the response will drop off as the campaign continues, you can in part compensate for this by taking a larger space for the duration of the campaign, and advertising less frequently.

Colour will increase the rate of response to your ad just as upping the size will. It is however more expensive, and people who are reading a black and white newspaper will be quite happy to respond to a black and white ad; its value largely depends on the standard for the publication. If everyone else's ads are in glossy colour, it is more important that yours should be too.

The position of your ad is also important, although it isn't always worth paying for the very best positions (which are the front and back covers). You will need to cost out the campaign to see if this is going to be worthwhile for you. In general, the best positions are:

- front cover followed by back cover;

- nearer the beginning of the publication;

- right hand pages rather than left;

- facing editorial but not surrounded by it;

- positions next to TV listings, letters or horoscopes;

- outside edges of pages rather than positions near the central fold.

All these may be worth testing, since both the product and the publication can influence the best positions, but you should find that these guidelines are fairly accurate for just about any product.

Inserts

Inserts are loose-leaf advertising inserted into a newspaper or magazine, or someone else's mailshot. They are, in a sense, a cross between press advertising and direct mail. The guidelines for designing them are the same as for direct mail material.

- They have the creative scope of direct mail, since they can be anything from a single sheet to a folded leaflet or a catalogue.

- They can be printed in colour even when inserted into a black and white publication.

- Press inserts have the broad reach of press advertising, so they can be used for high volume advertising.

- They have the cost benefits of press advertising, compared with direct mail.

- They are as highly targeted as the publication or mailshot they are inserted into.

- On average they cost four or five times more than advertising on the page, but they draw five or six times the response.

Tip-on inserts

It's worth mentioning this specialized kind of insert since there are one or two particular guidelines for using them. Tip-ons are inserts gummed on to an advertisement within the magazine. You might, for example, take a full page ad and attach a tip-on card at the bottom with your hotline number, asking the reader to peel it off and keep it by the phone. Or you might tip-on a sachet containing a sample of your moisturiser or your flower seeds. Here are a couple of tip-on tips:

- Make sure that full page advertising in that particular publication works for you before you start spending your money on tip-ons.

- Make sure the ad works without the tip-on, in case it falls out, or the first reader removes it and someone else then reads the ad. The usual solution is to print a coupon underneath the insert.

Television advertising

Television advertising is most often used to raise awareness of products and organizations rather than for direct marketing. But sometimes a TV ad will ask you to make a direct response by picking up the phone to place an order or ask for more information. It is also useful for supporting other direct marketing campaigns: 'Look out for our ad in your local newspaper this week.'

The other popular use of direct response TV advertising is for lead generation: 'To find out more about our luxury replacement windows, call . . .' The response rate to this tends to be low, so it is only worth doing if you have a high value product to sell. Its advantage is in putting a number in front of someone who has already decided they need replacement windows – you have saved them the bother of finding a number.

TV advertising can be very expensive, but the ability of sound and moving pictures together to influence people is beyond the capability of virtually any other medium. And as far as the cost is concerned, TV ads may be hopeless for reaching a specialized audience, but they are a very cost effective way of reaching a mass market. In the UK, you can advertise either nationally or in one or more of the 13 regions which the TV companies organize their advertising sales into.

The fact that you use direct response advertising on TV gives a particular impression of your company. It makes you appear approachable and friendly, with a desire to be accessible to your customers.

You will need to find a professional organization to make the ad for you; such companies are listed in BRAD. You may find that a freelance or small production company has lower overheads and is therefore cheaper, but insist on talking to referees and seeing examples of previous work.

When and how to advertise on TV

If you want viewers to contact you in response to your ad, there are certain rules to follow (see Box 4.1).

There are also guidelines for getting the best out of giving the phone number for people to respond to:

- People are over three times as likely to respond to the ad if you say the phone number as well as showing it on the screen.

- Show the phone number for at least 15 seconds.

- Make sure the phone number occupies at least 10 per cent of the screen.

- Freephone (0800) numbers get a much better response than calls the viewer has to pay for.

One of the most important aspects of direct advertising on TV is being prepared for the response. Most people – over three quarters – will respond within 15 minutes of seeing the ad. Suppose the response rate is 0.1 per cent, which is good but not exceptional. Even if only a million people see the ad, you can expect a thousand phone calls within a very short time.

Can you handle it? On one occasion a company is recorded as having taken 1200 calls, and lost 54,000. They had hooked their number up to an answering machine.

BOX 4.1 GUIDELINES FOR TV ADVERTISING

- People are unlikely to buy a product off the screen if they can get it down at the shops tomorrow. The medium is best for unusual or hard-to-find products.

- Use TV advertising for products which can be fully demonstrated on the TV, such as a specialized food processor, chopper and juicer, rather than computer software.

- If you want to make sales as a direct result of the ad, it should last between 60 and 120 seconds.

- If you want to generate leads, the ad need only last 10 to 20 seconds.

- Audiences are most responsive between about noon and 2pm. After that they become gradually less responsive as the day goes on; a direct response ad is best shown on daytime TV.

- Responses are better to ads run in the breaks between low-attention programmes, not highly popular ones.

- People are more likely to respond to an ad run at the end of a programme than one run during a break in the middle of the programme.

- People respond most often to ads run on a Monday or Tuesday. Response rates gradually fall through the rest of the week, and drop dramatically at the weekend.

- The bulk of the orders are likely to start coming in after about five or six showings of the ad.

The cost of TV advertising

TV advertising time is bought in units known as TVRs (television ratings). These indicate what percentage of the total potential audience will see your ad once. So 50 TVRs mean that 50 per cent of the viewers in the region you are buying the time in will see your ad once. However, you can buy more than 100 TVRs. This doesn't mean that over 100 per cent of potential viewers will see the ad, but that some will see it more than once. When viewers are likely to see the ad more than once, these opportunities are known as OTS (opportunities to see). So if you buy 400 TVRs, this actually means that around 80 per cent of potential viewers will have five OTS. In general, a direct response campaign should aim for around 350 to 450 TVRs.

Radio advertising

Radio and direct marketing do not go together as well as you might think, for two main reasons. One is that radio lacks the visual impact of press and TV advertising; the other is that people tend to listen to the radio when they are in the car, in the bath, at work, or somewhere else which makes it difficult to pick up the phone in response to an ad.

However, radio does have its benefits. It is a very trusted medium, which rubs off on the advertiser. And local radio is also regarded as a good friend, again an image it does you good to be associated with. Radio is a very useful support for other direct media: 'Look out for our leaflet coming through your letterbox soon'.

Radio is also effective for business-to-business direct advertising. Many business people listen to radio stations with a high news content on their way to and from work, and a constantly repeated phone number will sink in – especially if it is a freephone number. Or the name will sink in and the listener can then look up the number when they are in the office. This is most useful for high price products where the response rate doesn't need to be huge to make the exercise cost effective; office furniture, for example.

Local radio is an especially effective medium for direct response advertising, either business-to-business or in support of other advertising or, occasionally, on its own. As an example of this, the average number of blood donors turning up to donate was measured in one survey. When advertising was being run (on Capital radio) the average number of responses per week/per area was over a thousand. Without radio support the average was below a hundred.

5

Direct Mail

■   Direct mail is a highly personalized form of communication, and a highly targeted one. It enables you to write individually to as many people as you like and, unlike an advertisement, to enclose as much material as you like explaining the benefits of your products or services.

Most people like receiving post, and the image of direct mail is far better now than it once was. People no longer view it as 'junk mail' if it is well targeted; that term tends to be reserved for mail that is of no interest to them. If you only mail people who are likely to want to know about your product you should get a positive response in terms of attitude even from the people who don't order. That gives them a good image of you for the next time you contact them. Only when you mistarget your mail will the reader be irritated by your organization. This chapter covers the following:

■   The power of personalization

■   The mailshot   ■

The power of personalization

Direct mail – addressed mail – has a better image than unaddressed mail. According to research it is seen as being three times as honest. However, if you are going to personalize your mailshots you had better get it right. Prospects are very unimpressed if you get their name or other details wrong. If you write to someone offering to put a weatherproof render on the outside of their house, they will be very unimpressed if they live in an old cottage whose best feature is its stone walls. They will think 'These people obviously know nothing about me'.

Laser technology has had a huge impact on the personalization of direct mail. It used to be possible to personalize the address sticker on the envelope and that was it. Then it became possible to start one letter 'Dear Mr Smith' and the next one 'Dear Mrs Jones', although it was obvious that the rest of the letter had been printed off in bulk first and these personalized details overprinted subsequently.

Now, you can personalize anything you want to. Suppose you have developed a child's pushchair with a motor in it which takes the effort out of pushing. You can write to parents by name (*Dear Mr and Mrs Smith*, or *Dear Mr Smith and Ms Jones*), and you can include a reference to the number of children they have, and even their age and sex (*With a two year old daughter, pushing a pushchair can be quite exhausting* . . .). You are limited only by the information you have on your database. You could include the child's name, and send out mailings a month before the child's birthday (*Now that Jamie is coming up to his third birthday* . . .).

Time was, you had to leave a gap in the original text to fit personal details into. If you wanted to say *This product will revolutionize the Smith household* you would have to leave a large enough space to be sure that the name would still fit even if you were writing to Ms Fortescue-Weatherbottom-Smythe. Which meant that if you were writing to Mr Wu his name would be floating in a huge white space. But with computerized laser technology you can expand or close up the spaces as necessary – the entire thing can be personalized.

This technology is known as APA (all-points-addressable), and is well worth taking advantage of. You can personalize almost anything, and print it in almost any typeface onto virtually any paper at just about any angle. The machinery will print logos, graphics, charts and graphs. You can personalize envelopes and order forms. You can include a table of the interest each prospect will make under your savings scheme, using a different initial investment as a sample in each case, according to the likely amount affordable by each prospect.

When you send out highly personalized letters using laser printing technology, you should expect to supply the printer with a suitable magnetic tape containing all the information they need. Once you have found a good printer who has the technology you need, they will tell you what they need from you and when.

Personalization on a budget

If you can't afford laser-printed personalization, there are other ways to personalize your letters. At least personalize the name at the top if you can (if you really can't, don't say *Dear Sir or Madam*, or *Dear Customer*. Just say *Hello* or *Good morning*). But beyond that, you can divide the mailshot up into groups – the more the better. A comprehensive database makes a huge difference here. For example, you could produce two letters, one for people with children under 18 months (*With a child still too young to walk round the shops* . . .), and one for prospects whose children are 18 months or over (*Just because your child can walk, it doesn't mean they can keep going as long as you can* . . .). Or maybe a third as well, for people with children in both categories. Or you could break it down further, and state the sex of the child.

As you can see, the more categories the more the price goes up, but the increments aren't huge, and the value of the personalization can be considerable. Only you can decide how many groups of mailings is the optimum number for you on your budget. You could even send out a mailshot each month to those prospects or customers whose child's birthday falls in the next month (*With your child's birthday coming up soon* . . .). You can also use this technique of breaking up mailings to contact people who order at a regular time, or to mail everyone who hasn't placed an order in the last six months. Apart from anything else, it is easier to deal with the responses than trying to handle the response to one huge mailshot all at once.

The mailshot

As we saw with advertising, the first stage in planning a mailshot is to establish your objective. Are you looking for orders? Enquiries? Responses to a questionnaire? Do you want your readers to phone for an appointment? Send back a form asking for more information? If you aren't clear about what you want, neither will they be. So decide what you want from your mailshot and remain focused on it while you are working on preparing the mailpack.

The letter

The letter is the centrepiece of your mailshot. This is direct *mail* after all; it is a form of letter. It may be nothing but a letter, or it may be a letter and several other items, but the letter is always the focus of the pack. So what should it say?

There are two main categories of direct mail letter; you could call them the hard sell approach and the soft sell. (Not that the hard sell is pushy and aggressive – it shouldn't be. But it is hard by comparison with the soft approach.) The hard sell is more like advertising, while the soft sell is more like a phone call. If you're not sure which is suitable, try this exercise: imagine you have only two options for communicating with these people. You must either advertise in a magazine (which you know they read) or telephone them. Which would you choose? If your choice would be the magazine ad, go for the hard sell approach. If you would opt for the phone call, write a soft sell style of letter.

If you are mailing 50,000 prospects about your motorized pushchair you would need to adopt the hard sell approach. But if you are writing to only 500 customers all of whom have bought prams from you in the last year, you would probably go for a softer approach. Let's look at them each in turn.

Hard sell

I've already said that this is rather like advertising in a more personalized form. So it shouldn't be surprising that the letter should follow the same AIDA format (Attention, Interest, Desire, Action) that we looked at in the last chapter. There are a few additional points to make, however:

Attention

- Grabbing attention is important; you're competing with a lot of other direct mail. (When it comes to business-to-business mail, managers receive an average of three pieces a day.) You can use an attention-grabbing headline between the greeting (*Dear Mr Smith and Ms Jones*) and the first line of the letter: *Do you sometimes wish that pushing a pushchair uphill was a little less exhausting?* Make sure the headline contains a benefit or an implied benefit.

- Send something with your letter to attract attention. Preferably something which encourages the reader to read the letter for an explanation. Maybe a fabric swatch, or a tiny microchip mounted on a card (so as not to get lost) which carries the words *How can something this small make such a big difference to the way you drive your car?* Or use an incentive like the ones we looked at in Chapter 3 – a prize draw ticket or a free gift.

- Put a special effort into the first line of the letter. Make sure it encourages the reader to keep reading.

Interest

- Focus on your USP, as you would in an advertisement. Make sure you mention it at least three times during the letter.

- Make the letter as long as it needs to be to say everything you want to, but no longer. If you go over the page, make sure you end each page in the middle of a sentence so the reader has to turn over.

- Use plenty of subheadings to break up the text.

- Include details of any guarantees you can give, especially a no-quibble money-back guarantee.

- Include plenty of testimonials – take advantage of the fact that you have more room than you do in an advertisement.

Desire

- We saw in the last chapter that you can help kindle the reader's desire by reassuring them on any points of doubt they may have: *The motor is guaranteed for two years . . . the safety lock guarantees that if you let go of the handle, the motor cuts out . . . all the motorized parts are well out of the child's reach* . . . and so on. But now you also have room to cast doubt on the wisdom of *not* buying the product: *The pushchair gets heavier as the child gets older . . . Grandparents sometimes find pushchairs hard to manage . . .* and the like.

■ If your objective is to secure orders, tell the reader everything they could possibly want to know. But if you want prospects to identify themselves so you can keep in contact with future offers – in other words you want a lot of enquiries rather than a few orders – don't give away too much, or there'll be nothing for the prospects to enquire about. You need to get the balance right. If you give away too little, they will lose interest or become suspicious. If you don't mention the price, for example, they'll assume it's high. But keep back details about the full range of designs or colourways, for example. Let them know there are more than you've shown, and you can give them all the details if they phone or send back the reply-paid card.

■ At the end of the letter, don't grovel. There's no need to be their 'obedient servant' or to 'humbly crave' their response. You're not asking for a favour. You're making a mutually beneficial offer.

■ Make sure the letter is signed by someone appropriate. If the job title underneath the signature is a very junior one, it may insult the reader – it implies they aren't important enough for any of your senior people to write to. If you're asking for major expenditure or a buying decision at a high level in the company (in the case of business-to-business mail) the letter should be signed by someone at director level. For lower cost items a job title like Customer Services Manager may be sufficient.

Action

■ Give the reader a reason to order or respond promptly – stocks are limited, last order date in time for Christmas is coming up, sale price only lasts for three weeks or whatever. If you are asking for enquiries rather than orders initially, offer a money-off voucher to anyone contacting you before a certain date, or a free gift even if they don't order, or entry into a prize draw (as we saw in Chapter 3). If people don't reply promptly, they may forget to reply at all.

■ At the end of the letter, after your signature, add a handwritten-style PS; this always helps the response rate, sometimes even doubling it. Use the PS to reiterate some important point which will inspire the reader to reply promptly: *Don't forget to order before November 28th in time for Christmas!*

Soft sell

The soft sell letter is different because it reads more like a letter to someone you know personally; often you will use it to mail customers whom you do know in person. It is suitable if a letter is the only thing you're sending out, and also ideal for selling products with a high price or a high quality image.

These letters also have a formula to follow, but it is not the AIDA format, although of course you will still need to catch attention, arouse interest, stimulate desire and generate action. But you do it slightly differently. The formula for soft sell letters is the SCRAP formula:

- Situation;

- Complication;

- Resolution;

- Action;

- Politeness.

This is a very simple five-step approach to writing a business letter designed to interest and persuade, so let's look at each stage in turn.

Situation

Start by outlining the current position which the reader, or the market, is in. But you want to capture and hold the reader's attention, so don't tell them something they already know. And don't make the classic mistake of beginning the letter *As you know . . .* it simply tells the reader that there's nothing new here. Try something like *The average parent pushes their child's pushchair over five miles every week.*

Complication

Now state why this situation isn't ideal: *So it's no wonder you feel worn out when you get back from the shops or from a walk.*

Resolution

This is your chance to tell them how you can resolve the problem you've just identified: *Our Motopush pushchair does all the hard work for you.*

Action

This is direct marketing, don't forget; you want a response. And this is where you ask for it: *Return the reply-paid card if you would like us to send you our full brochure and price list.*

Politeness

All you have to do now is round off the letter: *I look forward to hearing from you.*

The letter will need to be a little longer than this, of course, although it is best to keep it to one sheet of paper. You can run to both sides of the sheet, but remember to end the first side half way through a sentence so the reader has to turn over. Just because you're being friendly and personal, it doesn't mean you can leave out the important ingredients of any sales letter. Make sure you still include plenty of benefits, reassurances, and your USP of course. And you can still use a headline below the greeting, enclose a free gift or sample, and give them an incentive to respond promptly.

On the next page is an example of a soft sell letter, personalized by customer name, and by the age and sex of the child.

The rest of the package

As well as the letter itself, you will probably want to put other material in the package. This could include a brochure, a specification sheet, a price list, an order or enquiry form, a reply-paid card, an envelope, a free gift, a sample, prize draw information, free tickets and so on.

If you are using the hard sell approach, perhaps selling a low value item to a lot of people, you could have several brightly-coloured enclosures which attract the eye. You can print prize draw numbers on glittery gold paper, and seal them inside a separate envelope, and include a return form to claim a free gift. We have already looked at the creative side of this material in Chapter 3.

Dear Mr Smith and Ms Jones

Have you ever wanted to take the 'push' out of your pushchair?

The average parent pushes their child's pushchair over five miles every week. That's around 250 miles a year. It's no wonder you can feel quite worn out when you get back from the shops or from a walk. And now that your son is almost two years old, he'll be getting pretty heavy to push all that distance.

What's more, it'll be a while before he can walk very far without you taking a lot of the strain. However, a couple of years ago, another one of our customers was talking to us about just this problem, and it gave us an idea. Why not put a motor into a pushchair to make it do all the hard work for you?

Of course, it's not that straightforward, which is why it has taken us two years to develop, hone, test and retest the *Motopush*. We had to make sure it was comfortable for both you and your child. We had to incorporate all the usual pushchair features that parents expect, such as waterproof materials, sturdy wheels and the option of folding the chair up to put it in the car. Then we had to develop a really reliable motor that we could confidently guarantee for the first two years.

But above all we had to make sure it was absolutely safe to use. Which is why we covered all the motorized parts so they are out of your son's reach, and we incorporated a safety brake, so that if you let go of the handle, the motor automatically cuts out. And we asked the British Standards Institute to approve it, which they did without any modifications.

Finally, we wanted the *Motopush* to look good, so we found a range of durable and elegant washable, waterproof fabric, in five different designs. We put co-ordinated foam around the handle for extra comfort, and we made the all-weather wheels look as tough and as strong as they really are.

The enclosed brochure shows you the finished result. And although you'd expect to pay a little more for the comfort and convenience of the *Motopush*, at £179 it's not much more expensive than a good quality pushchair that would leave you to do the hard work.

If you'd like to know more about the *Motopush*, return the enclosed reply-paid card and we'll send you our full brochure and information sheet, which contains all the specifications, and colour photographs of the full fabric range. If you return the card before 31 March, we'll also send you a £10 discount voucher to use if you order the *Motopush* before the end of April.

I look forward to receiving your request for more information about how to take the 'push' out of the pushchair.

Yours sincerely

Emma Horton

Emma Horton
Managing Director

At the other end of the scale, a soft sell letter is more personal, and would be better including no more additional information than necessary – a brochure that incorporates prices, a separate order form and an envelope.

Generating a reaction

What you want to achieve from this exercise is a response from your readers, and you need to encourage them to take three steps: open the envelope, read the letter and the other material, and reply to you. There are various techniques for persuading them to do all three of these things.

Getting them to open the envelope

If the prospect never opens the envelope (which happens to around one in six pieces of direct mail) all your hard work and expense will be wasted. So how can you encourage them to look inside? Here are some ways to encourage people to open the envelope:

Hard sell direct mail

- Trail the contents on the outside of the envelope: *Your prize draw number is inside* . . . This gives away that it's a direct mail letter, and therefore doesn't work well with soft sell or business-to-business direct mail. But it can be a good thing for hard sell letters. Test it first on a smaller mailing and see how it influences your response rate.

- If there is a free gift inside, say so on the envelope.

- Brightly coloured envelopes can boost the response rate; test this on a sample to see if it works for you.

Soft sell direct mail

- The more personal looking the envelope, the more likely people are to open it. Top marks for this go to a thick white envelope with a handwritten address and a stamp. Obviously this is often unfeasible, especially with a large mailing, but in general:

- Handwritten addresses are best, followed by typed addresses and then printed addresses. Address labels do least to encourage the recipient to open the envelope.

- Thick packages are more intriguing than thin ones.

- Stamps are more personal than franking, which still gets a better response than Printed Postage Impressions, or PPIs. (If you send large quantities of identical envelopes or packages you can arrange with Royal Mail to preprint a PPI on the envelope or carrier in an approved design bearing your company's own serial number.)

- White envelopes are more likely to be opened than manila ones.

All direct mail

- Suit the envelope to the contents. If you are sending out an expensive, glossy brochure for a luxury item, don't use a cheap envelope. The envelope gives the first impression of your product – and we all know about first impressions.

- Remember that everything you do should suit your corporate image, as we saw in Chapter 3. This applies to direct mail envelopes as much as to anything else.

- Some companies encourage people to open the envelope by making it look like something else, such as a bill. This often does the trick, but the recipient may feel they've been conned when they find out what the envelope really contains, so use this technique with caution and test it first.

- If you have no enclosures you could consider using a postcard with the message printed in a script typeface; this can be very catchy. It is a technique commonly used by, for example, vets letting you know that your cat or dog is due for its annual booster vaccination. This is, of course, a form of highly targeted direct mail – you are being asked to respond by phoning for an appointment – and one with an extremely high response rate.

Getting them to read the letter

Now they've opened the envelope, you want to make sure they read the letter. We've already looked at how to write it, and all the general creative rules in Chapter 3 apply. But here are a few more points to note:

- Use paper of a quality that matches the image you want to project.

- Be wary of printing onto coloured paper unless it is a very pale colour

– it takes much more effort to read print that is against a coloured background.

- For hard sell letters, use a second colour – something fairly strong like red or blue – for headlines, subheadings and the PS. You can also use this colour to underline key phrases (*We are also offering <u>two free tickets to Wimbledon</u> to anyone who orders a tennis set before the end of May*). Don't underline more than three or four phrases to a page, however, or you dilute the effect.

- If you use colour on the page – a single colour or colour photographs – it will attract the eye. So make sure you add colour in the places you most want the reader's eye to go to.

- For a hard sell approach, bright strong colours engender excitement and interest. If you're going for the softer approach, you might be better off using earthy, softer colours which convey honesty.

- Indent the first line of every paragraph.

- If you want to appear personal, especially for soft sell letters, don't justify the right hand margin.

Getting them to reply

So they've opened the envelope and they've read the contents. You're nearly there, but the final stage is the most crucial. Here are a few tips for encouraging your readers to take action in response to your mailshot:

- Include a reply-paid envelope or one printed with a freepost address. Bear in mind that you only have to pay for the ones that are returned. For business customers you can get away without paying for them to reply, but don't expect them to write out an envelope – make sure the address is ready printed on it. By the way, you don't need to spend a lot of money on the return envelope unless you are going for a seriously high-class look.

- Make sure the envelope holds the order form (or other material you are asking the reader to send back) easily and without too much folding.

- Make the order form, questionnaire, enquiry card or whatever you want returned as easy to use as possible; make any instructions very clear.

- Design the return form to match the letter and any brochure or other inclusions.

- If you have personalized the return form by printing the reader's address on it, this saves them having to write it out.

If you enclose an order form, there are specific guidelines for designing them in the chapter on mail order (see page 112).

How should you ask your readers to respond? It doesn't have to be by post. It could be by phone, fax, e-mail or by visiting you at a shop or exhibition stand. Most people still prefer to reply by post, although the higher their social grade the more likely they are to respond by phone. Business people still marginally prefer post to phone, but only by a couple of percentage points.

It's worth knowing why most people still prefer to reply by post. The main reasons they give are (in order):

- it's cheaper;

- everything is in writing;

- there's no hard sell;

- there's no pressure;

- there's more time to think;

- it's quicker and easier;

- it feels more safe and secure;

- they don't like using the phone.

Fax can be a good option if your prospects have fax machines, but if you want them to respond this way, design a fax response form for them to use. This has been known to boost the response rate for some business-to-business direct mail by as much as 50 per cent.

A lot of people like the option of replying by phone because it's faster, so it may well be a good idea to give prospects a choice. However, some companies find that they get a better response if they ask for only post or only phone responses than if they give a choice of either. So once again, it's worth testing what works best for you.

The way you ask people to respond also has an impact on your image. A first class business reply envelope comes top in the ranking for what makes your company appear genuine and suggests your products are high quality. Any reply-paid response speaks better of your company than a response in which you ask the reader to pay. Second class business reply envelopes, freefone numbers and freepost envelopes rank second, third and fourth.

The response

It's essential to think about the likely response to your mailshot at the planning stage. You can ruin any good impression you give your prospects with the mailshot by messing up the delivery of their order, or taking a month to respond to their request for information. If you mail 50,000 people and get a modest one per cent response, that's still 500 replies. Imagine you mailed 100,000 and got a 10 per cent response, which is perfectly possible. That's 10,000 replies.

You need to have the staff ready to deal with the response, either standing by the phones or by the letterbox or fax machine. And make sure you have the stock to fulfil any orders, or any offers of free gifts that you have made. If you can't cope with the likely response to the mailshot, can you split it into several mailings and stagger them over several weeks or even months?

Response rates

How do you know what response to expect? Well, it isn't easy if you haven't any relevant experience to go on. Apart from anything else, it depends hugely on the quality of the mailing list, the creative quality of the mailshot, and the product or offer it contains. But broadly speaking an unsolicited mailshot should get about a one or two per cent response if it isn't highly targeted, and as high as 10 or 15 per cent if it is.

Apart from mail order, which we'll be looking at later, people respond most often (in order):

- to questionnaires;

- to prize draws;

- to invitations to attend a free event;

- to place an order with payment;

- to place an order without payment;

- to ask for a visit;

- to ask for information;

- to make a donation;

- to visit a retail outlet.

There are also other rules of thumb about response rates:

- Broadly speaking, the larger the mailing, the lower the response rate. This is probably because larger mailings tend to be less targeted.

- Generally, the more money you spend on the mailpack (assuming you spend it wisely), the better the response will be.

Testing mailshots

Test your mailshots to see how you can generate the best response. Even the experts do this because there's no other way of knowing what will work. Send out two mailings which are as near identical as possible except for one factor, and see which does best. If you vary more than one factor between test groups, you won't know which one made the difference. The most important factors to test for are:

- **Product variations**. Do you do better if you offer the pushchair rainshield, sunshade and cover separately, or as an integral part of the product?

- **Price and discounts**. Do you get a better response if you offer a 15 per cent discount for prompt replies, or is it just as effective to offer only 10 per cent?

- **Mailing list**. Try sending exactly the same offer to a list of customers from a childcare store and a list of mail order customers from a children's clothing catalogue and see if one is more responsive than the other.

- **Timing**. Are people more likely to buy pushchairs in spring or autumn? Does it make a difference whether your mailshot arrives on the doormat on a Saturday or a Monday?

- **Response mechanism**. Will you get a better response rate if you encourage people to respond by fax? Or if you make postal replies the only method? Or if you use a business reply envelope instead of a freepost one?

■ **Amount of material in mailpack**. Does it help if you reduce the number of bits that fall out of the envelope when your prospects open it? Or should you include more material?

■ **Creative**. Does the photograph of the orange and green pushchair generate a better response than the photo of the dark blue one? Does the five-page letter get a better response than the two-page one?

■ **Gimmicks**. Try out different free gifts or samples or offers against each other.

Make sure that nothing else interferes with the test mailings that might affect the results. For example, response rates can be influenced by:

■ extremes of weather;

■ special occasions (such as a general election or the cup final);

■ public holidays;

■ dramatic national news;

■ local catastrophes;

■ a surge in activity from your competitors.

Even if all the test samples have been equally subject to this sort of interference, you should still treat the results with caution.

And finally . . .

In case you're tempted to think that it doesn't make that much difference how you ask people to pay, what colour the envelope is, when you send out the mailshot and all the rest of it, here's a piece of research that should change your mind. It was conducted by the direct marketing guru Drayton Bird, who describes it:

> If you take *all* the factors that go into a direct marketing programme, remarkable differences can emerge, as I discovered a few years ago when we were launching a new financial product. We tested 12 different mailing lists, three possible purchase prices, two different ways of paying, two different times of the year, and several creative elements. The most

profitable cell performed 58 times better than the least – a result calcu-
lated to give anyone interested in return on investment a warm feeling
indeed.

Table 5.1 shows what the difference was between the best and worst
performing test cells for each of these factors in this particular piece of
research.

TABLE 5.1 Differences between test cells

Factor	Difference between best and worst
Mailing list	× 6
Offer	× 3
Timing	× 2
Creative	× 1.35
Response mechanics	× 1.2

6

Door-to-Door Marketing

■ The term door-to-door marketing covers all the unaddressed mail that comes through your letterbox. It is reckoned to account for at least a third of all items that fall onto UK doormats – over five billion pieces a year. That's four times as much unaddressed mail as addressed mail. It is less personalized than direct mail, and less targetable, but that isn't always a disadvantage, except in the field of business-to-business direct marketing, where door-to-door is not generally effective since you need to address your mailshot to a named person. In this chapter we will look at:

■ The advantages of door-to-door marketing

■ Targeting door-to-door

■ Distribution

■ How to make door-to-door marketing work

On the plus side, door-to-door can be far more cost effective than other forms of marketing and you can cover any number of addresses you like, from a few dozen to virtually every letterbox in the country.   ■

Advantages of door-to-door marketing

Door-to-door marketing has many advantages:

■ It can be highly targeted. As we shall see in a moment, door-to-door can be very highly targeted demographically so that your leaflets or samples are dropped through letterboxes of a particular type of household.

■ Its reach is predictable. Like direct mail, you know exactly how many people your promotion will reach.

■ It is flexible. There is a choice of methods of distribution, and creatively there is a huge range of possibilities, limited only by what will fit through a letterbox.

■ It is a highly cost effective medium; it is just about the only way to deliver samples at a reasonable cost.

■ It is a useful method of collecting feedback, either through coupons or through questionnaires.

■ It's reliable. The major distributors are trustworthy and will deliver your leaftets on time and correctly.

■ It has the option of the personal touch. You can use people to visit door-to-door to distribute samples or collect information.

Targeting door-to-door

The original image of door-to-door – and the one that still sticks in many people's minds – is that it is a low cost way to flood a mass market with leaflets. But it has developed hugely in recent years, and can now be targeted very effectively indeed. The targeting you can achieve with door-to-door is to do with lifestyle, rather than special interests (amateur astrologers, stamp collectors or classic car enthusiasts, for example), for which direct mail remains better targeted.

But door-to-door is one of the best ways of targeting lifestyle groups. The whole of the UK is divided into postcode areas, which are themselves subdivided. Take an imaginary postcode: AB12 3CD. If you distribute to everyone in the AB12 area, you'll take in about 2000 to 2500 households. If you were to distribute to everyone in the AB12 3 -- area, you would be targeting about 150 households; this is possible but rarely done since it doesn't tend to be cost effective.

There are other ways than postcodes of grouping households. They can be targeted according to:

■   TV or radio regions;

■   county;

■   specific urban areas;

■   catchment areas for specific stores, shopping centres, cinemas and so on.

And then there are other demographic systems which have been developed, which classify regions or localities by other means:

■   By neighbourhood types, using Census information, on the principle that people of similar lifestyles live in the the same areas.

■   By Census data combined with publicly available housing, demographic and financial data, to produce more specialized lifestyle groupings.

■   Cross-referencing databases to identify the type of people likely to buy your products, and then identify the neighbourhoods in which they live.

■   Using the National Shoppers' Survey to identify people according to where they shop rather than where they live.

This means that you can be very specific about your lifestyle targeting if you need to. Suppose you know that your product appeals to single men in junior managerial posts. Perhaps you market an economically priced aftershave moisturiser which tends to appeal to younger men who want to make a good impression at work. You can make sure that you only drop leaflets through doors in areas with a very high proportion of such prospects.

Distribution

Once you have decided to use door-to-door marketing, you'll need to decide which distribution method to use; there are three options, known as solus, shared and news delivery.

- **Solus**. This system means that your material is delivered on its own, which has the obvious advantage that it doesn't have to compete for attention with other door-to-door material. If you use the Royal Mail's Household Delivery Service your leaflet will be delivered at the same time as addressed mail. This is the most expensive form of door-to-door marketing, but the individual attention it wins your material may well be worth it. If you want to use personal callers to deliver your leaflet, samples or research questionnaire, it is the only way to do it.

- **Shared**. This is cheaper, because your leaflets are delivered at the same time as others. There could be as many as four others, but they are guaranteed not to include promotional material for any competing products. You can still target households from areas or demographic types that suit you, and you can deliver small samples in this way as well as leaflets. Shared delivery is scheduled on a monthly basis.

- **News delivery**. This involves delivering your material at the same time as weekly free newspapers. Around 18 million households can be reached using this method, and it can be checked by reputable operators to ensure that circulation figures are accurate. One of the advantages of this method is speed: you can organize a leaflet drop to millions of households within a few days using news delivery.

What will it cost?

The low cost of door-to-door distribution is its biggest advantage over direct mail; it typically costs about half as much for the same number of addresses. Not only is the method of distribution far cheaper than the post, but you don't have to pay for mailing lists, personalized printing or envelope-stuffing. Very broadly, you can expect to pay as little as £12–£15 per thousand for shared or news delivery, and from around £25–£30 for solus distribution, if you are delivering a standard leaflet. The factors which will affect the cost of the distribution are:

■   the method of delivery you choose – solus, shared or news delivery, or personal callers;

■   the supplier you use;

■   the size of the leaflet or package;

■   the quantity you want delivered;

■   the distribution area;

■   the targeting you use.

Getting your money's worth

You get what you pay for with door-to-door distribution, and there are frequent stories of large numbers of leaflets being dumped by unscrupulous delivery suppliers. It is well worth paying more for a reputable distributor, although of course you should shop around for quotes from reliable suppliers. Make sure you use a company that is a member of the Association of Household Distributors (AHD) since these organizations will have to comply with a stringent set of membership standards.

There are a couple of points you should check with any distribution company to make sure they are giving you the best service they can:

1   Ask about their network system. Find out how many area managers they have – the more the better – and make sure they are full time employees of the distribution organization.

2   Ask how they check that deliveries have been properly made. They should have a thorough, and preferably independent, system for back-checking.

How to make door-to-door marketing work

We've seen what door-to-door marketing is, and how it operates. But how can you make the most of it? The average household receives over four items of door-to-door mail each week so, as with direct mail, you have to work hard to stand out. Research has shown that effective door-to-door marketing has certain common characteristics (see Box 6.1).

Door-to-door advertising works particularly well when it is supported by other media advertising. This is one of the reasons that distribution by television or radio regions is popular – you can launch a TV or radio campaign and then drop leaflets or samples through letterboxes.

BOX 6.1 THE CHARACTERISTICS OF GOOD DOOR-TO-DOOR ADVERTISING

- The recipient must have one of two reactions immediately they see your material: either they must recognize the brand, or they must perceive some reward for themselves in looking at it further (or both of course).

- People respond well to rewards such as free samples and money-off vouchers. The less hard they have to work for the reward, the better.

- The type of material that recipients tend to discard includes material that is delivered frequently for products that are rarely bought, such as replacement windows, competitions and some mail order goods. People also weed out anything that is overlong, overcomplicated or confuses them.

- The material should have strong visual impact which relates to either the brand or the reward.

- People don't respond well to clever teasers, such as head-lines intended to intrigue rather than inform; these almost always arouse irritation rather than interest.

- Any other information should be brief and simple. Don't use long chunks of text, and don't confuse the reader.

Take the aftershave moisturiser as an example. You could advertise this on television, or in suitable magazines such as *Arena* and *GQ,* and then organize a door-to-door distribution of samples, using demographic targeting to reach single, young professional men.

Door-to-door also works well for supplying public information literature. If you want to warn everyone in the local area that you are building a new superstore and give them information about traffic diversions during construction, this is the way to do it. Door-to-door distribution is popular with local authorities and utility companies for this reason. The biggest door-to-door distribution operation ever was carried out by BT when they informed everyone about the new telephone numbers which were introduced in 1995.

Another application of door-to-door is for new product launches, and it is also used by mail order companies to recruit agents, and by financial services companies.

Being creative with door-to-door

Many of the creative rules for direct mail and other forms of direct marketing also apply to door-to-door. However, door-to-door material can be bulkier than advertising and even direct mail. You can put anything non-toxic through a letterbox that will fit, and the best door-to-door marketers take full advantage of this. One of the most popular techniques among any kind of grocery manufacturer is to produce a leaflet in the size, shape and packaging design of the product it is advertising. This means that the prospect will recognize the product when they see it on the shelf next time they go shopping.

You can even do this with samples; there are companies which specialize in producing sample packs which are miniature replicas of the real package. So you can produce a miniature tube of aftershave moisturiser which will imprint the image of the packaging on the recipient's mind.

There is also evidence that retailers do very well out of producing a magazine or catalogue outlining their products and highlighting any current offers. This can be delivered to households in the retail catchment area – to all households or to only those in areas which suit the retailer's customer profile. This can be repeated for every branch around a region or around the UK, targeting only those people who are likely to shop at that particular store.

Getting a response

Door-to-door can be valuable simply as a means of communicating directly with your prospects or customers. But what if you want your communication to be two-way? Perhaps you need to build up a list of new prospects to add to your database, or maybe you want more information to add to the value of your existing database, or you want to conduct some market research. Few businesses seem to get the best value they can out of door-to-door; in fact it can be used very effectively for all these purposes.

The big clue with door-to-door is the reward. People want an immediate benefit as a result of reading or responding to your material. So give it to them; but make sure they have to do what you want them to in order to get it. For years people have dropped advertising through letterboxes which included money-off coupons to be redeemed at a retail outlet. The idea is that once the prospect has been tempted to try the product, they will switch to it.

This may work, but some people will need to be encouraged a few more times before switching regularly – and how do you know who they are? A better approach is to drop the coupons through the door as part of the door-to-door advertising, but make their redemption conditional on the customer filling in their name and address. Hey presto! You have a list of everyone who has taken up your offer, and you can mail them again with offers on the same product or on other brands.

According to some research, about two or three per cent of coupons in magazines and newspapers are redeemed, while the level of redemption for door-to-door coupons is more like 12 per cent. So this can be an effective way to build up a database for future contact, perhaps through direct mail, mail order or telemarketing. Or if certain neighbourhoods give you a high response rate, it might be cost effective to continue communicating with them through door-to-door.

Delivering samples through the letterbox can be highly effective, as we have already seen, since people can see an immediate reward from using your package rather than binning it. Once again, you can include a coupon on the pack: *If you would like to keep your skin clear and smooth, fill in your name and address and use this coupon to claim 50p off your next 100g pack of **Swoosh!** moisturizer.*

Questionnaires can also be successfully collected using door-to-door. All you have to do is to make the reward very clear, and dependent on filling out the questionnaire: *We'll give you a 100g pack of **Swoosh!** moisturizer as a thank you if you'll fill out and return this questionnaire in the* *envelope provided*. Keep the questionnaire simple and fairly quick – no more than about a dozen questions to complete by ticking boxes.

If you want to conduct a more detailed survey, use personal callers to knock on doors in designated areas and offer people samples in exchange for information. One of the benefits of this is that the callers can restrict the offer to suitable people. For example, they only need make the offer of a *Swoosh!* sample to male professionals under the age of 30. It is also a useful method of distribution if the samples are too bulky to fit through the letterbox, such as rolls of quilted kitchen paper, or unsuitable in some other way; for example, sample bags of dog biscuits would be useless dropped through letterboxes, for reasons which ought to be obvious.

Summary

Door-to-door marketing is like unaddressed direct mail in many ways, but with significant differences.

■   It is suitable for bulkier packages and samples, and it can be far more cost effective than direct mail. It is, at the moment, possibly the most under-exploited form of direct marketing there is; many businesses use it, but few use it really well.

■   Door-to-door can be highly targeted demographically.

■   The key to getting a response from door-to-door is to offer the recipient an immediately visible reward, such as a money-off coupon or a free sample.

■   You can get a response from door-to-door by asking for something, such as details for your database, in exchange for the reward you are offering.

7

Mail Order

■ If you send out a catalogue of any sort with an order form, you are running a mail order operation. This can be a huge pit into which you constantly pour money, or it can be a highly profitable enterprise. This chapter is about how to make sure it is the latter and covers the following:

■ What you want to achieve

■ Let the seller beware

■ Your product range

■ Your prospects

■ The catalogue ■

What you want to achieve

Many of the rules for running a successful mail order business are the same as for other kinds of direct mail. You still need to catch the recipient's attention, and encourage them to keep reading the catalogue. You will probably also send them a letter, although you might print this inside the front page of the catalogue instead of on a separate sheet. The information printed about each product should follow the AIDA format just as an ad would.

But there are other things you also need to achieve with mail order. You want to persuade people to order as many products as possible, not just one. And to keep ordering from you regularly. And to keep the catalogue until the next update arrives on their doormat.

If you're thinking of setting up a mail order company, or starting a mail order arm of your existing business, or improving an existing mail order operation, the first thing to do is to look at other people's catalogues, especially ones you know are successful. Go through them and see what attracts your attention, what type of products they sell, what sort of corporate personality comes across. And see what kind of special offers they make, how they set out their order forms, whether they include a letter with the catalogue, what their delivery times are like, how often they mail out the catalogue and so on. Get on as many catalogue mailing lists as you can; not just for products in the same kind of field as your own, but for completely different ones as well.

And make a note of where you found out about the catalogue. Did it arrive unsolicited? Did you see an ad and phone up for it? Was it recommended or passed on to you by someone else? Did you pick it up in a shop? Was it inserted into a magazine?

Let the seller beware

If you're getting into the mail order business, you will have to carry out thorough research of this kind, and think hard about what you're doing.

You can waste an awful lot of money on mail order if you don't lay the groundwork properly. It can take around three years to start making money out of mail order, so during that time you need to spend your money very wisely indeed.

It's best to be realistic about mail order right from the start, so here are some facts which will bring you down to earth and, hopefully, prevent you from making a huge and expensive mistake starting up an operation that isn't likely to succeed:

■ It can take several catalogues before people start to order from you, although once they have started they are more likely to reorder. The likely response rate from an initial mailing is only about one per cent, and many of those may place very low value orders. This is why it can take so long to start making money. The response rate will be higher, of course, if you are using a really well targeted list, for example if it's a list of existing retail customers to whom you are now offering a mail order service.

■ You may well have to spend £1 a copy to produce an effective mail order catalogue. This makes mailing very expensive. Suppose you mail out 10,000 catalogues and get a one per cent response. You would need each order to average £100 in value simply to pay for the cost of the catalogues, before you considered the envelopes and the postage, let alone other costs such as order fulfilment. And profit doesn't get a look in.

■ In an average catalogue, only 25 per cent of the products are ordered frequently enough to make money. The other products will either break even or lose you money.

■ You will need to offer people a no-quibble money-back guarantee on most types of catalogue products – and a lot of people will return the goods. In the clothing catalogue business returns can be as high as 60 per cent.

Sorry to sound depressing, but it's best to be prepared. Having said all of that, some people do run highly profitable mail order businesses so it can be done – just don't fool yourself it's easy. Some experts say that you should spend the first year finding out what the right mix of products is, the second year attracting new customers, and the third year finding out how many of the customers place repeat orders. Only then will you be sure whether you have a viable mail order business.

Your product range

Before you can set up your mail order business, you must have a range of products to sell. So you need to know whether your products are likely to sell by post – some are more suitable than others. What would you buy through the post? Have a look at this list of products, and think about whether you might buy each one through the post or not (assuming you were going to buy it) – and if not, why not?

- self-raising flour;

- wooden children's toys;

- specialist gardening tools;

- furnishing fabric.

It's possible that someone might buy any of these mail order, of course, but in general it is difficult to sell self-raising flour by mail order because it is easy to buy it next time you pop out to the shops. By the time you've noticed you need it, you haven't time to wait for a mail order delivery. And fabrics are very hard to sell through the mail because people want to both see and feel them first before they decide to buy. The most effective way to do it would be to send out samples, but this is long-winded for the customer and expensive for you.

Wooden children's toys and specialist gardening tools, however, might sell very well by mail order. A good photograph should be enough to tell you whether each product is what you're after, and both product ranges can be hard to find in the shops – mail order could be very helpful for your prospects.

This illustrates two of the key qualities of a good mail order product – it should be hard to find elsewhere, and it should be something that people are happy to buy on the basis of a good photograph. Research shows three other important ingredients for a product to sell well by mail – each of your products should have *at least* one of the five:

1   hard to find elsewhere;

2   can be bought without touching or seeing it, other than in a good photograph;

3   seen to be unique;

4   less expensive than buying it by other means;

5   has a story behind it (like the *Motopush* motorized pushchair from Chapter 5, invented by a frustrated parent).

Costs and prices

Mail order products need a high mark-up in order to work. You need to cover your administration costs, overheads, promotion, printing and mailing costs, packaging and fulfilment of orders. As a rule of thumb, you will need to add on a 50 to 100 per cent mark-up on products – and still sell them as cheaply or more cheaply than your prospects could buy them in the shops. (This is one reason why products which can't be bought in the shops are often a good idea for mail order.)

Even if you follow these guidelines, you will still find that a huge number of products don't do as well as you hoped; you might recognize why or you may never know. The important thing is to drop a product as soon as you can see that it isn't selling. Don't be tempted to rewrite the copy for the next issue of the catalogue, or to take the photograph from a different angle, or just to leave it in for a little bit longer to see what happens. If it doesn't sell, it doesn't sell – and you won't make it sell. Just cut your losses.

Broadly speaking, if your catalogue is full of relatively high price items you can expect about a third of them to make a profit, a third to break even and a third to lose money. If you sell low price ticket products, you'll probably find that around 60 per cent of them break even and of the rest, half will be winners and half will be losers.

One other factor to be aware of with catalogues is that products can go out of fashion while you're putting the catalogue together, or the market for the product can change. You might decide to exploit the fact that American football is very popular, and introduce a whole range of related products into your sports accessories catalogue. Then the national television stations drop the live broadcast of American football and the demand for products drops off.

It's not like running a shop, where you can put umbrellas in the window one week, when the weather is bad, and sun hats the next week when there's a heatwave. You have to plan well in advance. You can predict when people will have summer holidays, Christmas, and Wimbledon; but there are a lot of trends and fashions that are hard to plan in advance. And, as we'll see in more detail later, it will probably take a good couple of months to produce each catalogue, if not longer.

Average order value

The golden figure you need to calculate when you run a catalogue business is the average value of the orders you receive. This is what it's all about. And your key aim should be to push this figure up and up. The industry average is more than twice what it was in 1990 – make sure you keep going in the same direction.

It is far more cost effective to make £100 out of one customer than £50 out of two. It requires only half the administration, mailing, printing and overheads, and reduced despatch costs. And since prospects cost money, how much better to be able increase your turnover from the same group of customers than to have to recruit new ones in order to up your profits.

Of course you want to recruit new customers as well, but concentrate especially on your existing ones. Once you know which products they want, give them more of the same. Keep testing out new ways to encourage them to order, and ask them what they like about your catalogue so that you can keep improving on it for them.

Whose products?

If you set up a mail order business from scratch, you have to get your products from somewhere. You could manufacture them yourself, or you could buy them in. Or you might have a product you manufacture yourself and others you buy in for your catalogue sales. For example, you might manufacture clothing to sell mail order, and buy in belts, hair clips, shoes and other accessories to sell alongside your clothing. If you set up a mail order operation attached to an existing business such as a shop, you will presumably have your own range of products already, either manufactured or bought in.

Wherever you get your products from, you need to consider what you will do about stock control when you start selling mail order. Your customers don't want to wait six months while you order in or manufacture the goods for them, and you can't afford to carry huge stocks just in case someone places an order for them. This is particularly difficult at the beginning since you don't know which products will be most in demand. But if you send out thousands of catalogues, you could find that you have very high numbers of orders – hundreds or even thousands – for the most popular items.

You may have to budget for warehousing for a lot of products, unless you can make or order in very fast. Another option might be to pass on orders to the manufacturer to dispatch direct, instead of ordering the products to come to you for fulfilment. However, you'll have to make sure that their packaging and delivery meets your standards.

The important thing to consider is your delivery times. How long should your customers wait for their order? Look at it from their point of view – if your system doesn't suit your customers you will lose orders. Very few people will quibble about a fast delivery time, but a slow delivery may be a problem with some products. Take specialist paint suppliers, for example, who successfully sell ranges of historic paint colours by mail. Once you've decided on the paint you want, you want to get on with the job. You don't want to wait four weeks for the paint to arrive – most of us aren't organized enough to choose the paint a month before we start decorating. So the suppliers usually deliver within five days, and can get the paint to you in one or two days if you're prepared to pay for express delivery.

If you are selling sofas, on the other hand, people will probably expect to wait for two to four weeks. So think about what the customers for your type of product are likely to want. There is one other possibility that you may need to cater for: some products need to be delivered on specific dates, so make sure you use a supplier who can guarantee to fulfil orders in time for you to send them out, or who dispatches on time themselves. This is most likely to apply if you encourage your customers to ask you to send a birthday gift through the post on their behalf.

Your prospects

So you have chosen the most promising products you can to sell in your catalogue. Who are you going to sell them to? For a start, be realistic about the number of customers you need. To run a profitable stand-alone mail order business (rather than a branch of a larger business) you will need thousands of customers. If you have very high response rates and a high average order value you might get away with as few as 10,000 customers, but most successful mail order companies have many more customers than that. So where are you going to find them?

The American expert Dick Hodgson says: 'Prospects are costs; customers are profit.' You need to use a list with as high a response rate as possible, because the catalogue can be so expensive that prospects who don't buy can cost you a small fortune. If you already have existing customers, this is often the best way to start off a good list. However, if they all live just around the corner they won't want to buy mail order. But if you have a shop in a city shopping centre with a large catchment area, for example, you might find that a lot of your customers would much rather order by post or phone than by coming into town. Harrods operates a mail order catalogue because it has so many overseas and out-of-town customers.

If you don't have a good customer list, what can you do? The thing that is least likely to work is buying in a mailing list. Mailing out catalogues is much more expensive than most other direct mail, but the response rates are no higher. The only time this is likely to work is if you can buy in a highly targeted list, such as subscribers to a specialist publication in the same field as your products.

If you run a plant nursery specializing in rare poppies, and it turns out there is an organization called the Rare Poppy Society, their mailing list might well be worth using. But if you are starting a clothing catalogue, it is unlikely to be successful if you simply buy in a mailing list based on postcodes or clothing store customers. In any case, it is very rare to build a successful mail order business based on a specialist interest; this sort of operation only really works if it is part of a larger business, or if you are trying to run a small business that employs only a few staff. You won't turn a specialist mail order company into a big business.

One of the best options if you don't have a good list – or if you do but want to expand it – is to advertise for customers. You could advertise in the Rare Poppy Society's newsletter, or put in an insert, instead of buying in their mailing list and sending out catalogues to everyone. It can help to incentivize the response: *Return this coupon and we'll send you a £5 voucher to spend on your first order worth over £15.* You can advertise in magazines and newspapers, or using door-to-door or direct mail in which you advertise the catalogue and ask people to respond to receive their free copy.

The other option for distributing your catalogues is to do it through a retailer – or through your own stores, as Habitat do for example. Or through supplements and magazines. If you choose the right store, or the right publication, this can be an excellent way to persuade new customers to identify themselves. It saves the costs of enveloping and mailing, as well as the cost of buying in mailing lists.

The catalogue

The interface between your products and your customers is your catalogue. It is the single item on which the success of your business now hangs. So you need to get it right. And the most important quality your catalogue can have is personality. We saw in Chapter 3 that you cannot help projecting a corporate personality in everything you do; make sure it's the right one for your customers and your products. You want your prospects to look at the catalogue and think, 'This is my kind of thing.'

The personality you project will depend on your product range, as we saw in Chapter 3. If you're selling unbreakable plastic picnic equipment in bright, fun colours you will be appealing to a different group of people from those you would attract if you were selling expensive, leather-bound copies of books by classic authors. But you still need personality. You will project this with words, pictures, colour, paper quality, size and everything else which you have to make a decision about.

Let's take the picnic equipment as an example. A photograph of four plates lined up and a row of four glasses behind it would have very little personality. But you could show the equipment laid out on a picnic blanket covered in thickly spread, generous sandwiches, and slices of mouthwatering chocolate cake. Or you could show a family eating from the plates, all laughing as a small child is in the act of spilling his orange juice with a look of alarm on his face.

When it comes to the text, compare these two possibilities. Which do you think has the most personality?

1   The set of four plates and mugs comes in four different colours and is made of unbreakable polypropylene plastic. The plates are 8" in diameter and suitable for a range of different foods from starters and main courses to sweets and cakes. The material is heat resistant so the mugs can be used to hold hot or cold drinks.

2   This set of four plates and mugs will brighten up the dullest day for a picnic. At 8" across the unbreakable plates are big enough to hold a generous helping of lunch . . . or chocolate cake! And the polypropylene plastic material is heat resistant so you can have a refreshing mug of tea without burning your fingers.

Your personality will determine the style of your text and your photographs. It will also determine whether you use expensive-looking paper, a large or small format catalogue, the cover design or photograph, the colours you use as backgrounds or borders, the typeface you use, the layout and so on. Every time you have to make a decision about any of these things, stop and ask yourself what your choice will say about your personality.

Designing the catalogue

The way your catalogue looks will affect its profitability. If you collect other people's catalogues as part of your research you'll see that there is a wide range of styles, but there are certain guidelines that all the good catalogues will follow. As far as format is concerned, A5 often seems to do better than A4 for consumer products, although A4 can give a more appropriate image for more upmarket products.

There are lots of variations on these standard sizes, and you can mail out more than one version to test which works best for you. But don't keep changing the size in mailings to the same customers or you will risk losing their instant recognition of your catalogue when it comes through the door.

One more point on the format of your catalogue: consider the cost implications of mailing it. The size and format you choose can affect the cost of envelopes and the weight for mailing, so make sure that a decision to change the format doesn't take you by surprise when it puts up other costs as well.

There is an invaluable five point formula to follow for catalogue design known as RADER, which stands for: Relevance, Authority, Distinctiveness, Entertainment, Retention.

- **Relevance**. Your catalogue must be relevant to the people you are distributing it to. It must be the kind of thing they feel reflects their own interests, personality and tastes, and it must contain products they are likely to want and be able to afford.

- **Authority**. No one is going to order from you unless they trust you and believe in your products. The size of your catalogue will suggest authority – thin flimsy catalogues are somehow less convincing. You need to look serious enough to be reliable and trustworthy. One of the things which stops a lot of people from buying mail order is that they feel they have no security. Once they've sent off the cheque, will they ever hear from you again? If they do but they aren't happy with the product, will you agree to take it back? Give the impression of being a organization that is as good as its word.

- **Distinctiveness**. Your personality should be distinctive or your catalogue just won't work. Don't risk your prospects confusing your catalogue with anyone else's.

- **Entertainment**. If your prospects don't enjoy your catalogue, they won't read it – it's as simple as that. And you're competing with the television, the newspaper, magazines and everything else they could be doing with their time. So make it entertaining to read.

- **Retention**. Many customers may not order for weeks or months. Or they may order within days and then place another order a few weeks later. But only if they still have the catalogue. It is vital that your catalogue looks good enough to keep.

When it comes to the detail of design, the three main aspects to consider are layout, photography and text. Here are the most important considerations for each.

Layout

- Variety is crucial to keep the reader's interest. Vary the number of products on the page, the arrangement of photographs, the size of the pictures and so on.

- Pick an average number of products to show on each page – maybe five on an A5 page or eight on an A4 page. That would give you, say, just under 200 products in a 24-page A4 catalogue. Having picked the average, don't actually have very many pages which show this number. If you're averaging five products to a page have two products on some pages and eight or nine on others.

- People look at catalogues in double page spreads, so organize it that way. If you have a catalogue of decorative products for the home, organize them into spreads for each room, say; products for the bedroom, kitchen products and so on. But don't be too predictable. Put unexpected products in some sections – you can include the same product on another page as well if you need to. So you might include beeswax candles in the bathroom spread, with text suggesting a candlelit bath to relax at the end of the day.

- And vary the spreads: as well as a section for each room, have a whole spread in the kitchen section for ice-cream making equipment – machines, knickerbocker glory glasses and spoons, ice-cream recipe books, ice-cream bombe moulds and so on.

- Create more variety with the occasional page which is very different. You could put in an introductory page for each section, with no product information but a beautiful photograph featuring products that are in the section, and a title. For example, you might have a photograph of a bedroom with a luxurious four-poster bed draped in your curtains and covered in your bedding that simply says *The Bedroom*, to introduce the section. Or you can create variety with the occasional page that is devoted to a single product.

Photography

- You must show products photographically; it's the only chance the reader has to see the product at all. You are already asking them to buy it without touching it or seeing it in real life; don't ask them to buy it without even a photograph. I only know of one successful catalogue which uses illustrations rather than photographs, and it succeeds for two reasons. One is that it makes a feature of the fact that it uses colour illustrations, unlike every other catalogue, and the other is that the illustrations are exceedingly beautifully and accurately drawn, and probably cost more than photographs would have done.

- Photographs should be in colour and not black and white. Only the most specialized products can get away without colour photographs, and often these would be better off with no photographs at all than with black and white.

- Don't try to save money by using amateur photography – it shows, and it does no favours to your image. If you want prospects to see you as a reputable, trustworthy, professional organization, you must use good professional photographs. If you really can't afford them, don't go into the mail order business.

- You should show virtually every product in a photograph, but you can get away without if it is only a variation. You could photograph a pair of gold earrings and then say *Also available in silver*, or a pack of freezer bags and say *Available in the following sizes* . . . But be sure that people wouldn't rather see the product. If you show a blue cushion and say *Also available in green* the reader will need to know what shade of green, and only a photograph will tell them.

- Equally, if you are selling a set of four wicker baskets, you would do better to show them all, because then you can demonstrate the size rather than merely stating it in figures; you can show a flannel and a bar of soap in the smallest and a copy of a broadsheet newspaper in the largest. That way, you've also put into the customer's mind the idea that these baskets can be used in the bathroom, or as an alternative to a magazine rack, and so on. You can say a great deal like this with photographs rather than text; don't waste the opportunity.

- Go for plenty of variation in the photographs – use close ups and long shots, squared-off pictures and cut-out photographs, large and small photographs on the page (but don't make the small ones so small that they get lost or important details disappear). Cut-out photographs look very smart, especially against a white background, and can give your catalogue an elegant, upmarket image if that's what it needs. They also give visual variety since the outline of each photograph will be different, unlike squared off photographs.

- Think about the best way to photograph the product to help the reader. Does the reader need to see it from a particular angle? Would it help if you showed it in action? Should you show someone using the automatic bean slicer? Would the scale of the rug be clearer if you showed someone standing on it? Does it make more sense to see the children's climbing frame from a distance? Does it help to show a close-up of the double-security locking mechanism on the filing cabinet? You can always use more than one photograph for some products if that's the best way to give the reader the information they want.

- Use people in some of the photographs for the personal touch (they can also be very useful as an indicator of scale). But don't overdo it.

Text

- As well as injecting personality into the copy as we saw earlier, make it interesting by telling a story or posing a problem and then giving the answer: *What do you do with all those irritating left over pieces of soap at the end of the bar? Here's one way to wash your hands of them: just put them all in our new Soapmaker machine, and in 20 minutes you have a brand new bar of soap.* Good copy really is essential to the success of your catalogue. If you don't have a flair for copy writing, employ someone who can do it well. It will be money well spent.

- Give at least one or two benefits in the text for every product.

- Follow all the guidelines in earlier chapters for making copy readable. Use headings and subheadings. Print in a clear, readable typeface and don't try to print in white on a black background, or in any colour against a background that isn't light and easy to read.

- Make sure you include all the information the customer could possibly want. Is it machine washable? Are batteries supplied? Is it dishwasher-proof? What operating system does the software run under?

Where to put the products

Positioning is very important in catalogues – certain positions sell more products than others, because they catch the readers' attention most. You'll have to decide which products you want to promote hardest, and use these positions accordingly. The best selling positions are:

- the front and back covers;

- inside the front cover;

- the right hand pages, the earlier on in the catalogue the better;

- the centre spread.

Products which are promoted on the order form itself sell extremely well, so don't waste this space – use it to catch people's eye as they are filling out the form. You will also attract people's eye with a looseleaf sheet featuring special offers, summer bargains, end-of-line products and so on.

The covering letter

Always include a covering letter with a catalogue; it's friendlier and more personal. It doesn't need to be more than a brief letter on the inside page, but it should be there. Or you can print the letter on a separate sheet. Use it to emphasize any new products, special deals and so on.

Incentives can work very well with mail order so long as they are conditional on ordering, and you should draw attention to any incentive in the letter as well as on the order form: *There's £5 off all orders placed before 31 July* or *We're offering a 15% discount on orders over £100.* If you make an offer which is dependent on the value of the order, make it dependent on a value a little higher than the average order value, so as to push this up. If your average order value is £87, offer an incentive to spend £100. If the average is £44, incentivize orders of £50 or over.

The order form

This is a crucial part of the design of your catalogue; people can be put off ordering at the last minute if they aren't happy about the form, or if it's too confusing to fill in, or if they can't find it. So here are the most important guidelines:

- Make sure the order form is idiot-proof. Find a few idiots of your acquaintance to test it on before you go ahead. However simple you make it, someone will still get it wrong.

- Fill in the first line of the order form as an example (marked 'example'). Use this kind of order form, where customers fill in the blanks for themselves, rather than the type which lists every product with a box against each for the customers to tick if they want to buy it.

- You have to work from this order form once it is returned, so check that all the information you need is there, and laid out in a way that is easy for you to use.

- Some people forget all the rules of catalogue design when they come to the order form. You still have to make it match the style and personality of the catalogue, envelope and any letter you include.

- It's often a good idea to include two order forms: one which is part of the catalogue (either at the back or in the centre), and one separate looseleaf one. This means that if the loose one is either used or lost the customer can use the other one as a replacement or to place another order. Make the most of any spare space on the looseleaf form to promote seasonal items or special offers. Repeat any special deals on both order forms.

- Put your address on the order form in case your customer loses everything else.

■ Make sure there's plenty of room for people to order lots of items from you, and a 'quantity' column so they can order more than one of each.

■ Print clear details of any postage and packing charges.

■ Print a code on the order form which changes for each batch of catalogues so that you can tell which mailing this order came from, or which magazine insert or retail distribution.

■ Include a space for customers to fill in details of anyone else they think might be interested in receiving a catalogue.

■ Enclose a reply-paid or freepost envelope for your customers to use. Remember, you only have to pay if it gets used.

■ Print your fax number and your phone number (preferably a freefone or lo-call number) on the order form to give the customer a choice of responses.

Other ordering information

Your customers may want various pieces of information about your system before they order, so make sure you tell them everything they need to know. Include a page or a half page, preferably near the order form (because that's where they'll look for it), which tells them:

■ your phone and fax numbers for ordering;

■ what time of day you take phone calls (9am to 5pm, or 24-hour ordering, or whatever);

■ your customer enquiry number if it is different;

■ your delivery method;

■ your delivery times;

■ any express delivery option;

■ overseas delivery details;

■ what happens if they're not happy with the product when it arrives;

■ any guarantees;

■ specialist information (such as sizing for clothing catalogues, or information on how to use or care for the goods).

When to mail the catalogue

It's expensive mailing out catalogues, so you don't want to do it more often than necessary. But if the mailings are too infrequent you will lose potential orders – you need to keep your name in front of your customers and remind them that next time they want to buy an ice-cream maker or a bedspread it's worth taking your catalogue off the shelf (where they stored it because it looked too good to throw away).

As a general rule, you should send out your catalogue three or four times a year, but you may want to experiment with sending it out more often, or sending out a shorter catalogue of summer offers or Christmas gifts in between times, or mailing more frequently to those customers who order most frequently. If your product is more specialized you might find that fewer (or more) mailings work better for you. Garden bulb catalogues, for example, are usually sent out only twice a year, once in the autumn and once in the spring. If you specialize in Christmas gifts you may only mail out in October.

Producing the catalogue

It takes time and money to produce a good quality catalogue, and the golden rule is to prepare thoroughly and then ban any changes once the production process has started. Of course, there will be some things that unavoidably have to change – printing problems will crop up, or a product will have to be dropped after the page has been laid out because the supplier goes bust. But if the attitude is that changes are permitted you will spend a fortune on them every time. Whereas once people have grasped that they can't change their minds once the process has begun, they will make more effort to do their thinking in advance next time.

Broadly speaking, the main stages are photography, artwork, print preparation and printing, in that order. You should allow for photographing three pages worth of material a day, so it will take about 16 days to photograph a 48-page catalogue. Your designer should be able to prepare four pages of artwork a day on a typical catalogue.

When it comes to costs, paper will probably be the single biggest cost, amounting to as much as a third of the total. Photography is the next highest cost – about a quarter of the final bill – followed by printing, typesetting and artwork, and then repro (print preparation). When you work out your budget, add on about a fifth again for contingencies.

When you reprint your catalogue, you will not necessarily have to redesign every page or re-photograph every product. You will want to make some changes so that the reader doesn't look at a page, think 'I've seen this before' and turn over without another glance. But you can use the same photographs in different layouts, or reprint pages from time to time in amongst new pages. If you want to mail the same catalogue as before, which can attract new orders, you can simply change the cover design so that the customer doesn't instantly realize that they have seen the catalogue already.

Summary

Mail order can be very profitable, but you have to put a lot of money and care into getting it right or it can waste you a fortune. The key points to bear in mind are:

- It will take around three years to make money from mail order – or to find out if the venture will fail.

- You need profit margins of around 50 to 100 per cent.

- You need thousands of customers, and you'll need to use your own or find them by advertising; bought-in lists almost never work.

- Keep your eye on the golden figure – the average order value – and find ways to keep pushing it up.

- Remember RADER: Relevance, Authority, Distinctiveness, Entertainment, Retention.

Telemarketing

■ The word telemarketing describes any form of marketing using a phone; not only selling. Telemarketing can be a valuable part of both sales and customer service, and it can also be used to support other forms of direct marketing activities. This chapter will look at all the most common applications of telemarketing:

- selling;
- order taking;
- renewing contracts;
- enquiry handling;
- customer care;
- mailing list maintenance;
- research;
- supporting other direct marketing activities;
- complaint handling;
- building customer loyalty.

The telephone is a more powerful tool than the mail very often, since it allows for direct communication and conversation with your customers and prospects. This makes it extremely valuable for you, enabling you to ask and answer questions, reassure or remind customers, and use more sophisticated, verbal techniques for selling and research. It is a crucial part of direct marketing, and as you can see it has a huge range of applications. ■

Selling

Selling is a huge subject, and not one that there is room to cover here in detail, so I won't attempt to cover the basic techniques of researching the customer, handling objections, closing the sale and so on, which apply to any form of selling, with or without a telephone. However, there are some aspects of selling over the phone which are worth looking at.

The first of these is the cost. Teleselling (where you initiate the call) is far cheaper than putting a salesperson on the road, but it is still more expensive than you might think. The average cost of an outgoing call is between £5 and £15. This is because you have to pay for the staff, their training, the equipment, overheads, administration, and all the time wasted on calls which don't get through. You will need to work out the cost to you more accurately than this broad guide if you are going to budget your teleselling operation accurately.

The number of calls you can expect to make in an hour is also lower than many people realize, because of the time it takes to get hold of people on the phone (especially businesses where you need to get through to the switchboard and then the extension, and maybe past the secretary as well), and then the time the call itself takes. But as a rule of thumb, you can get through about ten consumer calls in an hour and perhaps two or three calls if you're selling to business decision-makers. Of course, not all of these will necessarily result in successful sales.

Sales techniques

When it comes to sales techniques, there are certain things that differ between face-to-face and telephone selling. Here are the most important things to remember:

■ You have less time to spend on a telesales call. Face-to-face sales appointments can easily take half an hour, maybe more, whether you're selling vacuum cleaners to consumers or photocopiers to businesses. But on the phone, no one expects a sales call to last longer than 10 to 15 minutes at most. So you need to go through the same process quicker.

- If you launch into a sales call with a closed question (one which requires a simple yes/no answer), you make it very easy for them to finish the conversation before it has started. If you sell promotional Christmas gifts for businesses to give their customers and you start by saying 'Do you give your customers a Christmas gift?' it is very easy for your prospect to say 'No'. Start with an open question (which can't be answered so briefly): 'What do you do about giving Christmas gifts to your customers?'

- Even once you're into the call, people find it much easier to finish a phone call than a face-to-face meeting. It's easy to say 'I'm sorry – I've got to go. Bye.' If you don't want your prospects doing this to you, you have to work doubly hard to keep their interest.

- Body language is important in face-to-face meetings. You can't use this over the phone, so you have to put extra effort into non-verbal communication, working harder to put warmth, friendliness and confidence into your voice.

Renewing contracts

As well as using the phone to generate new sales, you can also use it to generate repeat sales and contract renewals. Don't wait for the customer to call you, just in case they don't. Call them up and say 'You normally order another 500 XP30s at the beginning of September. We're only a couple of weeks away so I thought I'd call you before you run out and see if you'd like to place an order now. Is 500 still enough for you, or would you like 750 this time?'

When it comes to contracts, call them up about a month before an annual contract expires and say 'Your contract is due for renewal soon; are there any changes or additions we should discuss before we agree the renewal?'

What sometimes happens is that a customer is slightly dissatisfied with the service they get from you and is wondering whether to change suppliers or stop using your product or service. If you do nothing, they may never place the next order or renew the contract. But if you call, it might be easier to reorder than to take the trouble of finding someone new, and you will have another chance to prove yourself. If you're lucky, they'll tell you what their reservations are before they renew the contract or place the order, and that will enable you to improve your service to them next time.

Order taking

Order taking over the phone ought to be fairly straightforward. You apply the principles of good customer care (which we'll look at in a moment), you take down the details the customer gives you, and you ask for any information you need for your system.

What many people fail to recognize is that order taking is also an opportunity to do other things. Most importantly, it can be an opportunity to sell. If you buy a pair of leather shoes, the shop assistant will almost always ask you if you'd like to buy a can of leather protector spray as well. By the same token, you may well be able to offer your customer related products when they place an order. If they call up to order lever arch files, ask them if they need any dividers to go with them. If they want to order a sofa, let them know that you're offering 20 per cent off the price of footstools to anyone ordering a sofa this month.

Order taking can also be an opportunity to update your database. Assuming you enter orders directly on to your computer system, you should be able to check every time you take an order that the details you hold are correct. Not only should you always read back the address you have to the customer to make sure the order will be delivered to the right place, you can also check whether any other information is missing, or whether you hold two duplicate entries. You could say 'I've just noticed that we don't seem to have a phone number for you. Do you have a number I could make a note of in case we need to check your order details with you?' Or 'I seem to have two Mr P Smiths at your company, one in marketing and one in sales. Is that correct, or are they both you?'

Enquiry handling

Some of the phone calls which come in to your business are not actually orders but enquiries from potential customers. If someone calls up and says 'Do you sell these in green?' don't make the mistake of saying 'Yes, we do' and then finishing the call. This is a potential sale – don't waste the opportunity. Say 'Yes, we do. How many would you like?' and you're into a sales call.

You must be careful, however, not to bludgeon enquirers into buying. There are some lines of business where people expect to be sold to, and others where they need a very soft approach. If you phone up a stationers and ask if they sell lever arch files in green, you won't mind them asking 'Yes, how many would you like?' even if you're not yet ready to buy.

However, if you phone up a sofa manufacturer about a £2000 sofa and ask if they sell them in green, you might think it a bit pushy if they asked 'Yes, would you like to pay by cheque or credit card?' So judge your own business, and the tone of the person on the other end of the phone. But even if suggesting a purchase on the spot is overdoing it, you can always move one step further towards a sale, and try to get the prospect's name, address and phone number so you can contact them again to make a sale at the right time. If someone asks whether you manufacture a particular sofa in green, say 'Yes, we do; I can send you a swatch of the fabric. Can I take your name and address?' You're a step nearer to a sale, and now you know who the caller is to contact them later. Ask for their phone number as well, and call them in a couple of days to check they got the swatch . . . and now you're into a sales call.

Customer care

There are all sorts of ways you can look after your customers on the phone without actually selling to them – the aim is to build a good relationship which will be the foundation of future sales. You can check up on deliveries, answer technical problems, handle complaints and deal with questions about how the equipment works or when the delivery is likely to arrive. We'll look at complaint handling later in this chapter, but here are some pointers for other ways to look after your customers over the phone.

Telephone customer care techniques should of course be practised during every call of every kind, and we'll have a look at them in just a moment. There are a number of calls you might receive which are specifically customer care calls, not sales or enquiry calls. These include calls for information ('I usually buy these in packs of ten, but could I order just five?'), calls for advice ('I'm trying to assemble this wardrobe, and I can't work out how to get the back to stay upright while I put the sides in position'), and calls related to orders ('I ordered three of these last Friday. Can you tell me whether they've been dispatched yet, because I only want two now?'). The way you treat customers during these calls will have a huge impact on their attitude to your organization. Often the subject of the call is relatively unimportant; the way you handle the call is as important to them as the answer to their question.

Putting people on hold

The customer will start forming a view of your organization before you even answer the phone. If they can't get through to you, they will blame you for it. So make sure your customers and prospects aren't kept waiting to speak to you. You should employ enough people to be able to answer calls within about three rings.

What happens if customers can't get through first time? A lot of them never call back. They give up or go elsewhere. It depends on the reason for their call, of course, but research shows that only around a third of people surveyed would always call back to place an order from a catalogue. And over a third say they definitely *wouldn't* call back if they couldn't get through first time. When it comes to responding to an ad, only about one in seven say they would always call back. So how much business are you losing if your phones are engaged, or the extension people want is busy?

If you have to put people on hold, don't play music at them. It's the most popular queuing system for businesses to install, and one of the least popular with customers. What people want is not to have to queue, but failing that, they want to be told what their position in the queue is so they can assess for themselves whether it's worth hanging on.

Telephone techniques

Many of the rules for good customer care apply whether you are dealing with people face-to-face or over the phone. And some apply only to telephone behaviour. Here is a run down of the most important guidelines for all staff to follow every time they take a call – the most important components of a good call are:

■   **Speed and efficiency**. Answer the phone within about three rings (but not so fast you make the caller jump), give the company or department name clearly, and your own. Speak as though it's the first call you've answered today, not the hundredth, and avoid a sing-songy recitation such as 'Good afternoon, Universal Village Company, Sales Department. Pat speaking. How may I help you?' Try something a little more natural: 'Hello, Universal Village. This is Pat speaking.' Enunciate clearly and smile as you speak – you can hear a smile down the phone.

- **Helpfulness**. Sound as if you want to help. Face-to-face a customer can see you going to fetch the manual or calling up their details on the screen. But over the phone they haven't a clue what you're doing, so let them know. 'I'll just get your details up on the screen, and then I can see whether your order has been dispatched yet.' Nothing should be too much trouble, and the customer should feel you want to help: 'I can't tell you that at the moment, but what I can do is find out and call you back in the next ten minutes. Would that be all right with you?'

- **Politeness and friendliness**. Find out the caller's name, and use it. Never address them as 'caller'. It's impersonal to the point of being rude. Smile when you speak (not constantly but frequently), and make polite listening noises. People can't tell on the phone if you're listening, so let them know by saying 'Mmm' or 'Uh-huh' or 'I see' or by repeating back phrases to show you've been listening: 'You ordered it for Friday . . .'.

  One thing that creates a positive image in the customer's mind is treating them as an individual, and behaving like one yourself. That doesn't mean spending hours chatting on the phone, but the odd comment works wonders. If you're taking an address down you might say (if it's true): '. . . near Keswick? It's beautiful round there; I used to go on holiday there as a child.' If someone asks you to deliver before lunch because they're going out to take their driving test at one o'clock, call back later to see if the delivery arrived and ask how the driving test went. Or if a customer told you two weeks ago they wouldn't call for a while because they were off on holiday, ask when they return if they had a good time.

- **Product knowledge**. There's nothing more frustrating than calling up to ask how a self-assembly wardrobe that you're in the middle of failing to assemble works, and being told 'I'm not sure'. Or calling to ask which colours the lever arch files are available in and being told 'Black, red, blue, green, and possibly yellow, I'm not sure. Oh, and maybe not green, actually. And I think there are two shades of blue . . . or is that the ring binders? Oh, I forgot white. Or has that been discontinued . . .?' It's important that anyone who answers the phone should have a thorough knowledge of anything they might be asked about. And for the occasional call you really can't answer, don't dither. Just say 'I'm afraid I don't know. Let me find out. Would you like to hold for a minute or two or shall I call you back?' If you ask someone else to call back, or you put a caller through, tell them who they'll be speaking to: 'Can I put you through to Liz Baxter? She's our technical manager and she'll be able to answer your question.'

■ **Good follow up**. If you say you'll do something, do it. If you promise to call back today, call back *even if there's nothing to report*. Phone and say: 'I said I'd let you know today what was happening. I'm afraid I haven't managed to track down the courier yet, but I've left a message and as soon as I hear I'll get back to you. If they don't get back to me by five o'clock I'll chase them. Then I'll ring you again to tell you what's happening.' People want to be kept informed, so make sure they know as much as you do yourself.

   If you promise an express delivery, make sure it happens. If you say you'll get someone else to do something (make a call, arrange for a product to be customized or whatever) make sure they remember. Always keep your promises; the perfect phone call can still leave your customer dissatisfied if you don't follow it through.

One of the best rules for good customer care is to make a point of always doing that bit more than the customer asked for – going that bit further. That's what will make you stand out in their minds, and give them the feeling that they want to go on dealing with your company. If they ask you to phone them back before they go out at 5 o'clock, phone them back at 4 o'clock. If they want to know how the back fits on to the wardrobe they're grappling with, ask them if they'd like you to go through the rest of the assembly with them before they ring off. Every time you answer the phone to a customer, ask yourself 'What extra can I do that they aren't expecting?'

   And just one other word of warning about customer care: surveys show that for a typical organization two thirds of customers can be put off doing business with you again after experiencing a single badly handled call.

Carelines

A careline is a dedicated phone line for customers to ring for advice and information. It is generally printed on the product packaging, and may well be a freefone or local rate number. Carelines are useful for businesses which sell products that customers might want more information about. For example, if you run a travel company, a careline number printed on the folder for the plane tickets you send out would be very helpful. People can call to ask about maximum baggage weights, check-in times, meals on the flight and so on. A careline would be less useful if you sell A4 pads – customers don't tend to have a lot of unanswered questions about basic stationery.

If your business sells the type of product that customers might want to enquire about – whether you sell it directly or through a retailer – you should consider setting up a careline. And especially if your competitors use one. If the number is clearly printed on the packaging it can encourage people to buy the goods; they feel reassured that there is someone they can call if they can't work out how to programme the washing machine, or use the computer software.

Carelines can be answered by an answerphone, a voice-activated or tone menu system (a recorded voice saying 'If you want to enquire about operating procedures press five now . . .'), or a real person who can answer questions and give advice. Guess which of these options goes down best with customers. If you want to give the best service and encourage people to do more business with you, have a real person on the end of your careline.

You can also use carelines to help gather information for your database. Why not ask callers for their name and address? Plenty of carelines do.

Mailing list maintenance

You can check your database details by phone to make sure that your list is up to date. Suppose you're running a merge and purge operation. Sooner or later you'll have questions you can't answer by yourself. You might have a Mr Benet and a Mr Bennett at the same address. Which is the correct spelling? If you get it wrong you risk irritating the customer. But you might well wind him up if you always send him two of everything, as well as costing yourself money. So ring up and ask.

When you're checking business-to-business database details you should be able to get the information you need from the switchboard operator, or at least a secretary or an assistant, rather than having to disturb the contact in person.

Research

You can use the telephone to conduct market research by calling up customers, prospects and suppliers. This is obviously more time consuming than postal research if you are calling more than a very few people, but it does have many advantages.

When you send out postal questionnaires you need to ask people questions with a fairly limited range of answers. Often you supply the answers for them and ask them to tick the appropriate box. If you don't do this, it can be almost impossible to analyse the responses, since they won't fall naturally into groups. You can include a section that asks for 'any other comments' but many people leave this blank.

On the phone, however, you can ask anything you like. It's much easier to ask questions which might have very varied answers from different respondents, such as 'How do you find our delivery service?' instead of asking people simply to grade it on a scale of one to five. This gives them the opportunity to tell you why you haven't scored maximum points: 'It's fast and reliable, but the couriers you use are very brusque and unhelpful.'

One of the pluses of this kind of research is that people often can't think of anything to say when they're on their own with an 'any other comments' box in front of them. But once someone is there prompting them, they remember all sorts of things: 'Is there any other area of service you feel we could improve? How about our delivery service?' 'Oh, yes actually. That isn't as good as it could be . . . '.

Telephone research gives you the option of combining quantitative questions (the kind with finite, tick-box answers) and qualitative ones (those where answers can vary widely). You can start by asking people simple questions with yes/no type answers, and then go on to ask more in depth questions in the second part of the call.

If you haven't the resources to make all those phone calls, you could follow up postal research on the phone. If a lot of people tick a low-scoring box for your delivery service, you could phone round a number of them and ask the reason: 'You recently returned a postal questionnaire to us; thank you for taking the trouble to fill it in. We were pleased to find that our responses were mostly excellent, but several people gave us a low score for our delivery service, including you. We would obviously like to do something about this but we need to know exactly how our delivery service falls short. I wonder if you could spare a few moments to let us know what we can do to improve it?'

When you call someone to ask them questions for research, always start by telling them who you are and where you're calling from. Then explain what you want (and how it will benefit them) and check they have time to talk (tell them how long it will take): 'We're carrying out some research into how our customers feel about our delivery service so that we can make sure it is as good as possible. Do you have three or four minutes to talk, or could I call you back at a better time?'

By the way, don't do what some companies do and use research as an excuse to con prospects into a sales conversation. Don't survey them about what kind of kitchens they prefer and then say 'We have a sales-person in your area next week . . . '. This takes unfair advantage of the respondent's willingness to help with the survey, and will put off more potential customers than it recruits. Keep your research calls and your sales calls separate.

Supporting other direct marketing activities

The telephone is a useful adjunct to direct mail, direct advertising, mail order and door-to-door advertising. You will often increase your response rates considerably if you give people a phone number to call.

If people are responding to what they perceive as advertising – especially in the media or door-to-door – they are more likely to respond if the call is either free or charged at a local rate (such as 0345 numbers). However this is less vital if your prospects feel they are responding to a personal communication, such as direct mail or an addressed catalogue.

When it comes to direct mail, you can give your response rates a huge boost if you combine the mailshot with a telephone campaign. Many of your prospects are very busy. They may not even notice your mailshot or, if they do, they may simply never get round to replying even if they are interested. So call them. Let them know your mailshot will be arriving soon. Or ask them if they received it and whether you can help them further. Or both.

Research has indicated that the effect of a phone call on your response rates can be huge. The figures will vary from one business to the next, but as a rough guide:

- If the average response rate to a direct mail letter is two per cent, the response rate to a telephone campaign could be anywhere between two and ten per cent (of course it will be more expensive to run a telephone campaign, so you'll have to weigh up the costs).

- For the same campaign, sending out a letter followed by a phone call, or making a phone call followed by a letter, could up the response to 15 per cent.

- Best of all if you make a phone call first, then send the letter, and then follow with another phone call, your response rate can go up to between 10 and 20 per cent.

Obviously it can be impractical to make a phone call to every customer before and after your mailshot. It's fine if you're mailing a hundred, and not so easy if you're mailing 100,000. You can use an agency, but the costs don't necessarily justify this for supporting direct mail. However, you can always call the most promising prospects, or the best customers, up to the number you can manage most cost effectively. It doesn't have to be all or nothing.

What do you say?

If you're going to combine your direct mail campaign with telemarketing backup, you need to know what to say on the phone. There are two calls you might be making: one before and one after the mailshot arrives.

- **Before the mailshot**. The purpose of calling is to make sure the prospect notices your package when it arrives. So that's pretty much what you need to say: 'We have a new product out which can cut your printing costs by up to 15 per cent. We've put together an information pack which we'll be sending you next week, so I'm just giving you a call to ask you to look out for it.' The information pack is going to do the next stage of the work for you – you're simply arousing the prospect's interest enough to make sure the mailshot gets the opportunity to do its job.

- **After the mailshot**. You will have decided before you sent the mail-shot out what its objective was. To generate enquiries? To get orders? To set up appointments? To get responses to a questionnaire? This is the objective of this phone call as well – to finish off the job of the mailshot. Give your prospects about four or five days after receiving the letter before you call them – long enough to respond without the phone call if they want to, but not long enough to forget your letter. Then phone and treat the call as a sales call in which you are selling either the product, or the idea of making an appointment, being sent a full brochure, returning the questionnaire or whatever your objective was.

Call and say something along the lines of 'Hello Mrs Webster, this is Pat from The Universal Village Company; we spoke a couple of weeks ago. I hope you received our information pack in the post . . .' and then continue as you would for a sales call.

Supporting face-to-face selling

If you or your staff are on the road selling to customers by visiting them, you can save a fortune by incorporating some teleselling into your system. Suppose you visit each customer four times a year, and each visit is costing you around £200 (which is not unlikely, once you've taken into account travelling time, administration, depreciation on the car and so on). That means you're spending £800 a year on visits.

You may feel that you need to see your customers face-to-face, but what if you visited them twice a year, and called them between visits? You can tell them that you're changing the system to save them time, which it will do. The phone calls will cost you nearer £30 a time, making your annual expenditure – two phone calls and two visits – more like £460. That's a saving of £340 a year, plus a lot of time freed up to approach new prospects or do more planning.

If you think through all the visits you make, a lot of them do little more than wave the flag and collect a regular order, or set up the next appointment. As long as the customer or prospect can see the benefit for them, you can almost always replace some visits with phone calls.

Complaint handling

Many customers choose to make complaints over the phone rather than by letter. After all, they might have to hold a complex discussion or negotiation with you to explain the problem and get what they want, and that could take weeks by post. So the telephone is often the route they choose.

If one of your customers is unhappy, you want to do everything you can to help. And that means letting them call you up when they're unhappy if that's how they want to handle it. So you need to be well prepared to deal with complaints over the phone. In many lines of business, well over half the dissatisfied customers never complain at all; the figure can be as high as 96 per cent. That means you never get a chance to put the problem right. What's more, they will tell an average of 10 to 15 people about the experience they were unhappy with.

On the other hand, if you handle the complaint well enough, you can actually improve that customer's loyalty. You can leave them thinking that everyone makes mistakes, after all, but at least when *you* make them you can be trusted to put them right quickly and helpfully. They will tell fewer people about their experience, and what they do say will put your organization in a more positive light.

So you want unhappy customers to complain, rather than keep quiet about it. And there's one more reason to encourage them to tell you when they're unhappy. For every customer who complains, there may be 10 or 20 with the same problem who are saying nothing, just quietly switching their loyalty to one of your competitors. Unless you find out about the problem, this will go on happening. So the customer who bothers to tell you that your packaging is dreadful and some goods are arriving damaged is doing you a big favour.

Taking the call

It is very important that everyone who ever answers an outside call should be able to handle dissatisfied or even angry customers, even if all they have to do is keep them sweet while they pass them on to someone else. And you should have plenty of staff able to handle the call because if you put the customer on hold, they will sit and fume. And by the time you come to speak to them your job will be twice as hard.

You also need plenty of people who can handle complaints because it is crucial that someone sorts the problem out as soon as possible, and without the customer having to call back. According to research, the more often the customer has to get in touch with you to resolve the problem, the less likely they are ever to recommend your company to anyone else. And we're not talking about dozens of calls. If the customer has to contact you twice instead of once it can reduce the chances of their recommending you by 40 per cent. And a third call from them can halve the likelihood again.

The speed with which you respond is also vital. Customers recognize that it may take a while to ship out a new filing cabinet to replace the one that you delivered in the wrong colour. But they want to know as quickly as possible that that's what you're going to do. One organization discovered that when they asked complainers how satisfied they were with the way their complaint was handled, 70 per cent of those whose problem was resolved within four hours were completely satisfied. Of those who had to wait over four hours for a solution, less than half that number were completely satisfied.

So you need to respond quickly, and you need to respond without the customer having to call you back. But what should your response be? There are seven stages in dealing with complaints:

1   **Listen**. You need to know what the complaint is before you can deal with it, so let the customer speak first. But listening achieves more than just this – it gives the customer a chance to let off steam and feel that they have had their say.

2   **Sympathize**. Let the customer know that you recognize their frustration, anger, disappointment or whatever. Deep down, many people are worried that you won't acknowledge their feelings, which is why they start out on the defensive. So reassure them that their feelings are reasonable. However, don't apologize if it isn't your fault. Saying 'That must have been frustrating for you' or 'Oh, dear!' is not an admission of blame.

The rule for apologizing is simple: if it isn't your fault, don't apologize. If it is, do. Many people say that for legal reasons you should never admit blame or you could be liable for replacing the faulty goods or compensating the customer for late delivery or whatever it is. Well, so you should, and why not say so? The only exceptions to this are where the customer has suffered personal injury or financial loss. But if you delivered faulty goods you ought to be replacing them, so there's no harm in saying so. Do you want to hold on to your customers or don't you?

3   **Don't justify**. It doesn't matter whose fault it is. It's no good saying 'The instructions are clearly printed on the label; you can't have read them properly.' The aim is to resolve the problem, not to allocate blame. So avoid any discussion of whose fault it is. Simply let the

customer speak, show sympathy for the problem and then shift the focus of the conversation on to how to resolve the problem.

4   **Identify the options**. The customer wants to feel in control of the situation; if they are angry, handing them control will take the wind out of their sails faster than anything. So offer them a choice of solutions, and if they don't seem satisfied ask them to suggest what they would like to do. Try something like: 'Would you like a replacement or would you prefer to send it back for us to repair?' Or 'Shall we return your cheque, or hold on to it until you've received the goods?' If they're not happy, ask them 'What can we do to resolve the problem for you?'

5   **Agree a solution**. The customer may want to vent their frustration on you, but in the end they wouldn't have rung unless they wanted a solution, so find one that you can manage and which suits them, and make sure you're both clear about what is happening: 'I'll arrange delivery again for tomorrow, and I'll let the driver know you are going out at 11 o'clock so he's to arrive before that. And I'll call you back before 5 o'clock today to confirm that it's all arranged.'

6   **Take action**. Do exactly what you have agreed, and make sure anyone else involved (like the delivery driver) understands the importance of seeing the solution through.

7   **Follow up**. Contact the customer after the problem has been resolved and make sure everything went smoothly from their point of view and that they are now satisfied.

One piece of research asked members of the general public what factors they considered most important in handling complaints. Their answers included (in order of importance):

- speed of response;

- being kept informed;

- friendliness and helpfulness;

- having a named person to deal with.

Building customer loyalty

We all know – or we should by now – that retaining existing customers is less costly and more effective than recruiting new ones. (Recruiting new customers often costs as much as seven times as much as hanging on to the ones you've already got.) So one of the most profitable marketing tactics is increasing the loyalty of your existing customers. And the phone is an excellent tool for doing just that.

You want your customers to know that they matter to you; that you care. Most of us call our friends every so often to say 'We haven't spoken for a while. I was just calling to see how you are.' We should do the same with our customers. It's usually easier to find a reason for calling, but the object of the exercise is not to sell to them; it's just to let them know you care.

Don't wait until something goes wrong to contact your customers. You can call after a delivery to say 'Did everything go all right? Were you happy with the service we gave you?' Or you might ring to say 'We gather you've merged with another company. Should we be writing to you at a new address, and has your ordering system changed?'

If a customer has ordered a product for a special event – a launch or an anniversary party or the opening of their new branch – call them up afterwards to ask how the event went.

You might ring to promote a special offer, but don't hard sell, and pick suitable customers to contact: 'We're introducing a discount service for customers who spend more than £200 a year with us. Since you're one of our best customers, I thought it might be helpful to tell you about it.' Only contact people who do spend over £200 a year with you, and of course those who spend almost £200 – to push up their order values a bit further.

Nobody wants to be pestered on the phone constantly, but a phone call once or twice a year helps your relationship with your customers no end. You may be able to personalize your direct mail, but they know deep down that they're not the only one receiving it. But a telephone call is genuinely one-to-one, and it shows your customer how important they are to you better than anything.

Index